Happy Mind, Happy Life

A Science-Backed Guide to More Happiness and Self-Love

Barbora Centik

Please send all requests, questions, or feedback to hello@8bcpublishing.com
We are happy to hear from you.
https://www.facebook.com/8BCpublishing
https://www.instagram.com/8BCpublishing

ISBN 978-3-949152-04-7 (paperback)
ISBN 978-3-949152-05-4 (hardcover)

For me,

my family,

and my second family—my friends.

Table of Contents

Welcome to Happiness

Clap along if you feel like happiness is the truth
Clap along if you know what happiness is to you
Clap along if you feel like that's what you wanna do

~ Pharrell Williams (Happy)

While we all know and relate to these famous (and viral) lyrics, we may not always experience this concept in our daily lives. What is happiness? How do we get it, and why is it so vital that we have it?

We all want to feel happy. Like the words to a famous song, we want to sing through life, yet we often end up feeling miserable and living a less than stellar existence. What is happiness to you? You probably have your own definition of what happiness is. Most people don't really agree on what constitutes it. When we're unsure of what something means, we grab a dictionary or google it. The *Oxford English Dictionary's* definition of happy, which is "feeling or showing pleasure or contentment" (Simpson & Weiner, 1989), does seem to help a little. So, to feel happiness, you need to have pleasure and be content, but is that also *your* definition?

Your happiness might include things such as having enough of that which you need, being with people who make you feel good, having mostly positive experiences, and living a pleasant life. Perhaps you have this; maybe you don't. If you are happy, you may feel blessed, but what about if you don't know what real happiness is in your life?

Maybe you live each day wondering what the point of life is when you don't feel pleasure or contentment? You may know the pain of being unhappy or unable to give yourself the love you need, the peace of mind you desire, and the sense of accomplishment that comes from reaching your goals. Basically, you may be stuck on the deserted island that your life has become.

This book is your boat off that isolated island, and it is taking you to a future filled with what you need, the skills you desire, and the concepts that will help you find your inner happiness. Happiness is a state of mind. Happy minds make for happy lives.

Happiness is contentment with who, what, and where you are. It shouldn't be confused with joy or pleasure. Those are transient states connected to things, experiences, and people. Happiness is about you—how you feel inside and how you experience the world. Time to open up and invite happiness to come from within you and (ful)fill your life.

Can You Become Happier?

If happiness is something inside you, and you can't get it from outside sources, how can you get more of it? It may seem like a secret, but happiness (or at least the potential to have it) comes from within us. Science points towards the potential that everyone has to explore this inner source of happiness through strategies like specific happiness-driven activities, gratitude work, and practicing kindness.

This book is not going to make you any promises. There are enough lies being sold out there; instead, it will give you a research-based view on what happiness is and strategies how to actively achieve it. It will help you find and understand known activities that can help you (re)discover happiness and stock up that internal happiness spring that you were born with. This is where I come in.

Why I Can Help You

I used to be an anxious person prone to depression. My days were not happy, and my personality almost caved under the pressures of trying to live like that. However, I set out on a mission to find out what happiness was and how to achieve it. I devoured research papers, trying to see what science had to say about happiness. I had never been a touchy-feely type of person, and while I found benefit in mindfulness, I wanted hard facts and research studies. Perhaps I secretly wanted to discover that some magic vitamin deficiency was the root of my problems (it wasn't), but I discovered a clear series of steps to achieve my happiness instead.

After analyzing hundreds of research papers, scientific articles, and studies, a process of trial and error followed, and one day, I realized I had changed. I had blossomed from being that anxious little birdy into a brightly singing gal. (Okay, so I don't really sing, but you get the point, right?) From what I had learned, I began helping my family, and they, too, improved and became happier, and I thought, "Alright, so I'm onto something here."

Next, I started sharing the knowledge with my wider social circles, eventually creating a ripple effect of happiness blossoming in the minds and lives of those who learned what I had to offer. The idea for this book was born, and it is my hope that I can spread this science-based knowledge in a practical way to those who read this.

I will be completely honest with you—I struggle to stay content from time to time. Such is life. But through the strategies I'm going to share with you, those days became rare. If I could rediscover my inner happiness, turning myself from an anxious Annie into a charismatic Carla through a scientific process, then so can you.

How to Use This Book

If you've chosen to read this book, chances are that you are feeling unhappy about something (or everything) in your life. This book is a guide, but you have to do the work. It is not some magic pill that will instantly make you smile and feel all fuzzy inside. Instead, it is a roadmap to help you discover your inner self, build the mechanisms for achieving *your* happiness, and facilitate the tackling of larger issues you may not have been able to face until now.

Each chapter is designed to give you the essential knowledge about happiness as it applies to you. I will share what I have learned about money, your body as the birthplace of happiness, relationships, kindness, gratitude and being present in your life, honesty, and the setting and reaching of goals. Once you are fully prepared with this knowledge and have begun to interpret and internalize it into yourself and your daily life, you can begin to refill your happiness well.

As I'm humming along to Pharrell's happy song, it hits me with the catchy lyrics: "Clap along ..." Happiness is something you work at, and it requires action. You have probably tried working on yourself and searched for happiness before (after all, nobody likes being unhappy). Change doesn't just appear in your life; it isn't magic! I can give you the knowledge I have discovered and researched, but in the end, it is up to you to clap along. It is up to you to sing along and find your happiness. Without YOU doing the WORK, nothing will happen. You aren't alone though; I'll help. In my own meandering searching and questing for happiness, I discovered some amazing facts and ideas about happiness. They changed my life for the better. What I have learned, I share with you here. I have walked the road, and knowing the steps that brought me to my inner wellspring of happiness, I can now share that process with you as you grow your happiness, improve your well-being, and develop a brighter view on life.

Happiness is not something for the select few to enjoy. You can change your life and know the taste of inner contentment through the systematic process in this book. In fact, you may be surprised by some of the amazing things science has discovered about the nature of happiness and the ways in which you can achieve it. This is an exciting journey, and you should start it right now!

What happens if you don't? Nothing. Yip, nothing changes if you don't give yourself the chance to create real and lasting happiness. If you don't keep working at this system, you will once again postpone working on yourself, and you will continue to lack contentment. Happiness isn't going to rock up in your life like a long-lost relative who's come to make you wealthy—it takes work!

"Clap along if you feel like that's what you wanna do!" Yeah, you need to feel like you want it. You must want happiness. The rewards of being happy are untold: health, success, better relationships, and a longer life... Who wouldn't want that?

Chapter 1

Everyone Can Learn to Be Happy

The foolish man seeks happiness in the distance.
The wise grows it under his feet.

~ James Oppenheim

"I am so blessed to be so happy," a friend once told me. While I swallowed a healthy dose of envy, I realized that this was such a mistaken concept. Happiness isn't some blessing you get for being a good girl or a smart boy. It's something you work at and achieve. It's a little like going to the gym every day and finally having a summer bikini body. You do not magically wake up and slip into your skimpy bikini and look awesome. It takes work, hard work. Happiness takes work—it is a learned skill. It is not a reward but a destination.

Are You Born with It?

Babies laugh a lot, and since we may mistake that for happiness, it has created the concept that we are born happy (forgetting that babies also cry a lot!). So, what happens to make us unhappy in later life? Did someone take our happiness?

These questions cast some light on how we view happiness. We tend to see it as something outside of us, something we either have or don't, something we're born with and lose, or something that is taken from us. None of these views are correct.

While it is true that some people are born with a predisposition towards joy and seeing the brighter side of life, it doesn't mean that you may have been born with or without happiness. Instead, happiness is something you cultivate.

The opposite of happiness would naturally be depression. Studies into the genetic nature of depression are still in its infancy, although depression is known to run in families. This begs the question whether depression is a result of nature or nurture (MedlinePlus, 2020).

Similarly, what is the origin of happiness? Is it a result of nature (as in genetics) or nurture (as in learned)? While science can point out that certain elements of your biology contribute to happiness, such as having the correct serotonin levels, it can't pin down where happiness lies in your body or mind.

Hence, happiness isn't something you have or don't have; instead, you create it every day. It requires a conscious decision to achieve a higher state of inner well-being and positivity.

How Your Personality Influences Your Happiness

Happiness is such a widely debated topic that a field of psychology specially aimed at the study of happiness has developed—positive psychology. Proponents of this field of study have declared that happiness is something you work at.

Personality may be a large hindrance to happiness if you suffer from a neurotic or introverted personality type. This is partly due to these personality traits fostering a negative world view and creating a victim complex (Pishva et al., 2011).

Your personality may influence how and if you experience happiness. Extroversion or outgoingness of character, conscientiousness, as well as mental and emotional stability, seem to contribute the most to your experience of happiness. While it may be easier for people who have these personality traits to experience contentment, it is not to say you require this to feel happy. Instead, you can feel happy if you are a neurotic or introverted personality type person—it's just going to take some work.

People predisposed to having a happy "nature" tend to find happiness more easily, or at least, that's the perception. Research has found that happiness is less about being an extroverted person and more about being assertive in what you want (Pishva et al., 2011). When you stand up for your needs, requirements, and desires, you are more likely to have what is known as an internal locus of control, which is vital for happiness to thrive. This means you take ownership of your life, not blaming others or holding outside forces responsible for your actions or what happens to you.

We have already stated that happiness is something you create. You do not ask anyone's permission or blessing to be happy. Instead, it comes from you. When it comes to happiness, you are its creator. Placing yourself in the driver's seat is key to achieving happiness. Whether your personality makes you naturally assertive, or you are introverted and hide from the world, your ability to assert your will is what determines your happiness.

Can You Trick Your Brain into Happiness?

So, what to do when your brain is already unhappy? Can you trick your brain into feeling happy when it isn't really happy?

On a biological level, your brain is a magnificent organ, and it is able to change and improve in a dynamic way known as neuroplasticity. This adaptability of the brain's neural tissues allows for your brain (or mind) to rewire itself to enable a better quality of living. So, while you may not have been born happy, you can create new pathways towards happiness in your brain.

How does this work? Your brain forms new connections and deeper pathways based on concepts such as repetition and adjustment. It means, if you can fake happiness enough times, you can form these paths in your brain to create the message of feeling happy.

Your brain can be trained (which is perhaps a more positive and structured word than to say it is tricked) into forming habitual thoughts and connections between the different parts of the brain that connect to happiness. This allows for increased serotonin (the happy neurotransmitter) production, which will, in turn, improve your happiness levels by stimulating good moods and positive thinking.

While you may be wondering at this point why you haven't carved out craters towards happiness by now, it should be pointed out that neuroplasticity has its limits. Although you can make a few moves along the emotional scale towards being happier, it may not be realistic to expect that you magically transform yourself into happy Harry overnight.

In reality, you need to engage in activities that strengthen and build the neural pathways between the nucleus accumbens and the prefrontal cortex in the brain. These are responsible for feelings of gratitude, optimism, and hopefulness (Corcoran, 2015). Joining a gym (and developing all the structures associated with feeling good, since physical activity also triggers the release of endorphins) is one way to start working out those neural pathways.

There are several ways to encourage your brain to become happy, and this book will delve into some of them in more detail, but I want to point out two ways that worked at fostering a sense of happiness at the start for me: gratitude and learning to wait.

Gratitude is such a huge thing that I have devoted a further section to it in this book, but right now, I want to mention delaying gratification. We live in a consumer culture where everything is constructed around the principle of "right here, right now." This has led us to be unable to wait. We want fast food, quick money, easy friendships, and even our babies are photographed ad nauseam while still in their mommy's belly (in the old days, we were content to see the baby once the little one popped out).

In a culture of wanting rewards right now, of being unable to wait and losing the ability to persevere, is it any surprise that happiness has fallen by the wayside? We struggle with waiting for anything, even for good things, and this has destroyed our enjoyment of simple things, which is one of the fundamental pillars of happiness.

Window shopping activities become shopping sprees as we struggle to contain ourselves, and we live off credit cards when we are dissatisfied with our real income. Mistakenly, we believe that we need money (and more of it) to buy things to make us happy. The reality is that money and things will not fill the hole in your soul.

If that sounds way too dramatic, just consider this: have you ever bought yourself something simply to "cheer" yourself up? Happiness is not about cheering up. It is about having contentment regardless of where you are, what you own, who you know, where you think you belong, or whether you are "important."

Happiness is more of a skill than a state of mind. Tricking your brain into feeling happy is the result of the diligent management of your thoughts and behavioral patterns. In essence, you can fake it to feel it. Gordts (2014) writes that happiness is a skill that can be learned. This means, just like you learned to walk and talk, you can learn to manifest happiness in your life. So, how happy are you right now?

Where Do You Rank with Happiness Right Now?

While we seem lost without an app or a prescription to help us in life, some introspection can help you establish your current happiness baseline. Note that this is only a starting point, not the final say on whether you are happy or not. Your happiness is not an all or nothing condition; it is rather a large sliding scale ranging from being utterly miserable at one end to being filled with warm contentment and assurance every day at the other end. Most of us operate somewhere in the middle, and the goal is to avoid sliding towards the negative side of the spectrum (although on bad days, we may dip into those murky waters) and rather edge towards the positive side of the scale.

Happiness Questions

1. Do you share your thoughts and feelings with those close to you?
2. Do you believe in doing nice things for others?
3. Doing things that challenge you is a satisfying experience, true or false?
4. When you look back at your life, do you have a sense of gratitude for the events that brought you here?
5. During the day, are you focused on what you are doing? Or do thoughts of the past or the future distract you often?
6. Can you list five things you cherish in your life without needing to think in depth?

While there is no wrong or right with these questions, they guide you towards a deeper understanding of who and what you are. This is what each question reveals about your happiness at present:

Q1: When you feel like you can't share, you often doubt your significant others and also yourself. Your happiness will be dimmed when you don't feel confident enough to open up to your loved ones.

Q2: When we are happy, we tend to do things for others. Our inner joy seems to spill out and touch everyone around us.

Q3: When you have no faith in yourself, you don't see yourself as capable of achieving success. People who feel like this tend to avoid challenges since they expect failure. If you never challenge yourself, you are afraid of meeting your strength (or thinking that you have none, especially when you are depressed).

Q4: People who experience happiness know that their lives are the result of winding paths. Not only do good experiences contribute to who we end up as or where, but bad experiences also serve a function. When you look back, do you only see bad experiences and wish they never happened? You may be sliding down the happiness scale if this is the case.

Q5: Happiness is about now. You can't be stuck remembering happiness in the past (it's already gone), and you can't expect happiness in the future (you haven't felt it yet). When you are focused on here and now, you are living your life in the moment.

This moment is the only place where you can create happiness.

Q6: If you struggle with this question, you are struggling to feel gratitude. Without gratitude, your brain is wired to see negatives and lack, instead of focusing on what is real and precious.

These questions are simply aimed at getting your brain active and thinking about your life at this moment. For some, this may be too painful, and they struggle with doing six questions. Using an app to track happiness might help you ease into self-awareness and introspection. There are many apps to choose from for this purpose. Tracking your “happiness development” over time could also help you create more contentment as you realize your power to create it. It may seem a little artificial, but once you understand the advantages of this concept, you can benefit from the direction such an app can give you.

Now that you have a basic concept of the way in which your brain, your perspectives, and your biology can affect your state of happiness, it is time to confront your beliefs about money and realize that while you can’t buy happiness, money can be a vessel for happiness when used wisely.

Chapter 2

Beyond Money

Wealth is the ability to fully experience life.

~ Henry David Thoreau

There is a tribe—the Himba—in Namibia, Africa, who live entirely without money. They do not have any form of coin or wealth that is traded to establish some form of social standing. The only concept of social status is determined by how many cattle a person has owned in their life. Despite not having any monetary interest, these people are happy. When searching for information about the Himba, you find photos of smiling women, happy children, and wise yet contented men.

Perhaps the absence of a monetary system contributes to their happiness? Among the Himba, there are clearly defined roles. Priorities include maintaining an ancestral fire for each family unit, which burns 24 hours a day. Living in simple homes made from materials found in their environment, these people do not compete to make a bigger or fancier home than their neighbor, and they happily stand together as a community when there is a crisis. For these people, happiness is not tied to money, but it is about the people, their ancestors, and daily living or living in the moment. Could you live without money?

Does Money Make the World Go Round?

Most of us have heard the saying, "money makes the world go round." Is there any truth in this? Does the amount of money you have equate to your level of happiness? It comes down to the ultimate question: can you buy happiness?

While it is undoubtedly better to be rich and unhappy than poor and unhappy, money is only as important as what you spend it on. This does not refer to buying flashy cars or fancy houses, and you and your happiness may be better off when investing in experiences (as studies have proven—but more on this a little later). Money is only as good as what you invest in.

If you need any evidence of money not being able to buy happiness, just consider all the famous and rich people who struggle with depression and excessive lifestyles as they try to find happiness. Happiness can't be bought, or can it?

The Money Myth

A sad reality for many of us is that we have dreams of attaining a better job, earning more money, buying a flashy car, or going on an expensive holiday, and then we will be happy. This expectation means we make our happiness conditional upon getting more money. What happens when you don't get that money? Does that mean you will not be happy?

The internet abounds with stories of people who quit their jobs and worked for less money and became happier for it. Happiness doesn't have a dollar sign attached to it. Having some money can help decrease your stress, though. For instance, being able to pay your child's school fees or afford medical cover for your ailing parents can certainly take a mental load off, and this, in turn, can make you feel a certain sense of contentment.

Having it doesn't guarantee happiness, but when you are able to afford things that matter, it can contribute to your contentment. The key concept then is not making your happiness contingent on having money. When it comes to money and happiness, it is not a have or have not situation.

Americans have reported that a lack of money is their main cause for stress, while the close second is the lack of time in their lives (Hershfield et al., 2016). While money causes stress when you don't have enough to meet your needs, it is not responsible in itself for making you happy either. The above research study linked having more time as contributing more positively to happiness than having more money. This finding is interesting as we clearly want more time to do things than to buy things. Certainly, many people know individuals who earn big salaries, and these people often complain that though they have money, they don't have time to do anything that makes them happy.

While employers tend to offer a raise in pay as motivation to secure longer work hours, this is a poor incentive as most people desire to have more time to spend with their family and loved ones (activities that make them happy). When we can spend time connecting with people, we experience happiness, but when we spend time working (to earn money), this is an independent activity, and it contributes less to our overall happiness (Mogilner, 2010).

As a final point to raise, many people have found that when they earn more money, they tend to simply spend more, failing to save for that expensive holiday they really wanted. Having more does not guarantee financial freedom; just think of the celebs who run up debt that exceeds their personal finances and still end up utterly bankrupt (financially and emotionally). Jebb et al. (2018) reported that while high income is only associated with satisfaction but not happiness, extremely low income is associated with a lack of satisfaction and emotional distress among most people in America. People have a better sense of life value when they earn a bit more (up to $95,000 per annum), but after that, it makes no difference whether they earn more or less than that plateau amount. When it comes to emotional well-being, the above study found this to plateau at $60,000–$70,000 income per year. It would seem to suggest that there is a limit to how much money can improve your experience of happiness.

The above study also found that while there is a limit to how much money you need to be happy, developing countries require a lower amount. In contrast, more affluent countries only achieve happiness with a larger sum of money. This can be seen in some countries with a below-average income but where there is still a greater life satisfaction among the population. Conversely, some states with a higher national income experience lower life satisfaction when people earn more than the plateau amount of $60,000–$70,000 per year. The study, therefore, concluded that the amount of money that could make you happy has a limit, and when you cross that threshold, your life satisfaction starts to decline again.

Money and your experience of happiness are all about your mindset. Creating the correct mindset relating to money will help you develop a healthy and balanced life view.

Hedonism and Adaptation Theory

Hedonism, since it's often misunderstood, is when you believe in seeking pleasure to feel happy. It boils down to believing that the outside world is what gives you happiness. This means you place the outside world in charge of your contentment and happiness. When you follow this line of thinking, you then believe that buying stuff will make you happy, and while it probably does for a while, it does not have a lasting effect. But why does that just-purchased glow not last?

A theory known as adaptation theory stipulates that any living organism will adapt or adjust to changes in its environment and then consider these as being part of the normal. It is a survival mechanism: in the wild, if an animal suffers an injury or becomes altered in some way, that animal will adapt to the change and carry on as usual. If the animal had to stop and fuss over every little change, it would never be able to get on with living.

In humans, this trait—adapting to changes—makes us lose the glow of nice things. We may have a momentary thrill at owning a new car and spend a whole month cleaning every inch of that car, refusing to let people eat inside the car, and drive like we're driving Miss Daisy, but then the thrill wears off, and McDonald's is winking, and we want to get where we're going quickly. So, the cherished car becomes just another thing in our lives. We have adapted. Nothing has changed, and we plateau back to basic pleasure levels, feelings of malcontent, and despair (Pennock, 2020).

So, how do we make sure the things we spend money on will offer us lasting pleasure and add to our happiness? We use money as a tool to extend our efforts into happiness, not as happiness in itself.

The Generosity Effect

It's better to give than receive. Your parents most likely raised you with this belief, and while it was functional for getting kids used to the fact that life will probably take more than it gives (and you'll have to get used to not getting as much as you give), it is not untrue. There is more contentment in giving than receiving.

Being generous is a reward in itself. Seeing someone smile at receiving your gift or making someone's life just a little bit easier fills you with a sense of goodwill and contentment. Research has shown that people are happier when spending money on others than when they spend that money on themselves (Walsh, 2008). The amount of money you spend doesn't matter; it is more about who you spend it on. When you spend it on others, you feel happiness and inner contentment that far outlasts any momentary high from spending it on yourself.

Prosocial spending, or spending on others, has been proven in worldwide studies to stimulate a sense of deep appreciation and reward experience in people. This is known as a generosity effect (Aknin et al., 2013). It would seem that when you share happiness (through money), you experience it too. Even when you are told to spend money on yourself, it isn't nearly as satisfactory as spending on others. Studies have proven it's better to give than to receive.

When Money Can Buy You Happiness

So, can money buy you happiness? Here I speak not of spending on others but spending on yourself, and the answer is—yes. Confused? While I've been saying money can't buy happiness, it may seem like I've now lost the plot. Money can buy the experience of happiness, depending on what you spend it on. If you buy experiences and not things, you are using your money to facilitate happiness. How does this work?

Going out for some take-aways and milkshakes with friends every once in a while as a treat can give you happiness. You enjoy the company and the social experience. That experience is essential in life as it makes you feel less like you're isolated, and it helps you avoid social comparisons like who is driving the better car or who has the latest designer outfit. While we can compare things, we can't compare experiences. This makes experiences priceless, and happiness can be created like this.

Going out every day is not going to be nearly as satisfying as you may think. While social experiences are enjoyable, you also need to balance this with being happy in yourself when you are not in a crowd. Instead of the spending being about a dollar sign, it is about how that "buy" makes you feel. Experiential spending (buying an experience) is more satisfying and contributes more to your overall happiness than a material purchase (buying something). Things don't give pleasure, but experiences do (Kumar et al., 2020).

Even the thought of the experience is pleasurable to you. While you wait to go on holiday, you are already experiencing happiness and excitement. On holiday, you may find yourself in utter bliss, while returning home may be followed by a lifetime of memories that make you smile upon recall. Compare this to buying a pair of shoes, for instance. While you may look at the picture of the shoes online and fantasize about yourself wearing them on a date, chances are that the date is more memorable than the shoes. Swiping a card to buy those glorious six-inch stilettos may be thrilling, but tomorrow you will not feel the same way (certainly not when those shoes start pinching).

The process of recalling a lovely holiday or social experience is also likely to create feelings of gratitude, feelings you are blessed to have experienced, and you will feel inner satisfaction too. Thinking about possessions tends not to have the same effect. While you may be excited by a new leather jacket, you do not feel that sense of gratitude that comes with experience (Walker et al., 2016).

Spending money on people and experiences is a much better way to invest in your happiness. Not only does it buy you memories instead of price tags, but it also buys you a warm glow that only sharing can bring.

Finding Happiness in a Material World

While having money may in itself contribute to happiness, since it allows you to pay for experiences that create social memories, chasing after dollars will not make you happy. Those who are consumed by a pursuit of financial wealth do so at the cost of their emotional, mental, and social health. In the end, money chasers end up bankrupt despite having large bank balances. They have all the money they could want (although these people never seem to be content with the money they have), yet they are still wrapped up in the sense of lack.

In a material world, where we are constantly bombarded with imagery of sales, social media posts about the wealthy and affluent being happier, and where a culture of hedonistic pleasures abounds, it is so easy to believe money means happiness. However, research has proven that happiness is not about things; instead, it is about experiences and using money to help us feel content.

The anticipation of an experience such as a holiday with friends or imagining how a gift we have purchased for a dear friend will make that person feel, is far more satisfying than splurging on ourselves. Long term, this is a better investment as memories are forever, and we will never forget that feeling. These will far outlast any pair of designer shoes or even a flashy car.

In fact, excessively spending on yourself can even lead to your isolation from your social group and cause you to be ostracized by your peers. People are quick to judge someone who indulges in shopping sprees as being selfish, and they naturally gravitate away from them. Happiness can be facilitated by money, but it can never be bought.

While spending money on something today that gives you a momentary pleasure, that feeling will not last unless it is experience related. Soon, the thing you spent money on will no longer please you as much. Things only have value when we can use them to give us experiences of pleasure. For instance, buying a mountain bike so you can go biking with your friends over weekends can bring you happiness as this is about the adventure and the company more than it is about the bike.

In the end, the way we see money is greatly tied to our ability to use the money to facilitate our happiness. When we see money for what it really is, we can begin to use it to help us achieve happiness.

How Materialistic Are You?

Throughout this book, you will be taking control of your happiness. Part of this is self-reflection activities, action-activities, and creating plans for changing your view on happiness and creating more of it. I recommend you get a hardcover book you can journal in. You can invest in a special book or just grab a two-quire book off the stationery section—the results will still be the same: it depends on what you put into this experience, not on what you pay for the book.

1. List Your Purchases

This is an interesting self-reflection activity to do. You need to list all the material purchases you've made over the last month. It could include stuff like clothing, entertainment vouchers like Spotify or YouTube, morning coffee at Starbucks, or gym memberships.

Now, next to each, write whether the purchase was experience based or material based. For instance: a clothing purchase could be for a work function or because you really liked a jacket (since it looks just like the one J-Lo was wearing on the cover of People Magazine). This one is then a material purchase since it is tied to an item, not an experience. (However, if the jacket is so you and your friends can go to a J-Lo concert, and you all wanted to dress like J-Lo for the evening, then it becomes an experience-related purchase.)

You may have purchased some entertainment vouchers since you are lonely at home at night and want to be entertained, making this an experience-related spend. A purchase of your morning coffee could be in response to your being late for work and not having time to make coffee, or you could be buying coffee at that coffee shop since you enjoy speaking to the friendly salesperson at the coffee shop. The gym membership may have been purchased since you want to get into shape or because you enjoy attending group spinning sessions.

Whether something is experience related is dependent on sharing the moment with someone or creating memories with what you purchased. When you spend money on things purely to have them, you are not creating memories as these are material expenses.

Which of your purchases were experience based, and which were not? What does this reveal about your current spending habits? Are you trying to buy things and that momentary bliss, or are you buying memories? True happiness is experience based. Do you get your happiness from experiences or things?

2. Experience the Generosity Effect for Yourself

Look at your budget. Have you got any money that is not accountable for paying a bill or paying an essential? It needn't be a large sum. Even five dollars a week can be plenty for this challenge. Now, look at the people you interact with. Who among them (and it needn't be a friend or close confidant) could use a special cheering up?

Perhaps the receptionist at work looks a little down this week, or the homeless man you pass on the way to work looks hungry, or the taxi driver is more quiet than usual. These are the kinds of people who could use an act of generosity. You could buy the receptionist a donut when you grab your morning coffee, and when she's not looking, slide it onto her desk. The homeless man could use a warm meal as you pass him on your way to work (saving some food for him may not cost you much, but to the homeless man, it could be the only meal he has today). Leaving a tip for the taxi driver may bring a smile to their face and, in turn, warmth to your heart. These random acts of kindness can certainly go a long way to brightening up someone else's life as well as your own.

Having done your small act(s) of generosity, consider how it made you feel. In your journal, record a few of these acts of generosity and write how you were feeling. Record this feeling on the day it happened and then again a week after when you think back on it. Do you see any patterns emerging? That's the generosity effect.

When you consider the things you spend money on, you may have noticed that many of these you don't really need for a happy mind or a happy life. So, why are you buying them? What need do they fill? Perhaps it's time to look at the place where your mind and your happiness lives—your body.

Chapter 3

Your Body—Start with Your Mind's Home

Take care of your body. It's the only place you have to live.

~ Jim Rohn

Happiness is a state of mind, but that mind lives in a body—your body. Fat, thin, short, tall, healthy, unhealthy—this is where your mind lives. While you may think a mental state has nothing to do with your body, you would be entirely wrong. Science has proven that what happens to your body affects your mind. Physical illness can manifest in your mind, and mental illness can have a psychosomatic effect on your physical body too. To get control of your happiness, you need to invest in how you think about happiness and how your body contributes to it.

Healthy Body for a Healthy Mind

While a healthy body is often seen as one that is perfectly toned and appealing to the eye, this may not contribute anything to your mental happiness in the end. Instead, a healthy body is one that functions optimally in terms of the major processes such as excretion, respiration, sleep, exercise and movement, and nutritional intake. Just ask someone who suffers from irritable bowel syndrome how devastating this is to their quality of life. It will undoubtedly affect their ability to create a happy mental state.

When your body is not functioning as nature intended, you are not only risking your physical health but also your mental health. As soon as your cycles are out of whack, you are messing with body chemistry and natural processes designed to help you foster healthy thinking. You also risk sinking into depression. So, let's start with the most effortless process but also the one people struggle the most with—sleep.

Sleep

Just think of those days when you woke up after a good night's sleep. Can you recall just how you felt for most of the next day? You were able to deal with minor annoyances and simply smile as you moved on. There may even literally has been a spring in your step. On the other hand, whenever you struggle to get a decent night's sleep, you wake up the next morning feeling like death warmed up, and you are quickly upset over the smallest thing. Sleep is essential to creating happiness.

When you suffer from sleep deprivation, which is a consistent lack of enough quality sleep, you can begin to damage your body and negatively affect your mind. Watson and Cherney (2020) find that sleep is required to form new thought patterns. A consistent lack of sleep induces mood swings, and you are likely to be prone to irritability and could suffer a mental breakdown entirely. Happiness will not be likely when you are consistently sleep deprived.

Quality sleep has been connected to many remarkable discoveries as your brain puzzles at challenges during sleep while it creates new neural pathways. A good example of this is the creation of the periodic table by Dmitri Mendeleev who dreamed up the solution to this complex table. He woke up one morning knowing the answer (Wagner et al., 2004).

Sleep deprivation can also increase the risks of real threats to your body. You can become more likely to contract cancer, suffer obesity, and experience heart diseases (Kogan, 2020). Studies at Binghamton University found that a lack of sleep also leads to negative repetitive thinking (Kogan, 2020). Further studies confirmed that sleep deprivation led to emotional overload with negative emotions dominating your mental processes.

Other nasty side effects of interrupted sleep or sleep deprivation are diverse (Schocker, 2014). You could suffer weight gain, suffer a lower immune system, suffer decreased brain function, lose memories, increase your diabetes risk, and even risk death. Getting sleep is about more than just happiness; it's about having a quality life, if a life at all.

For adequate and quality sleep, you need to maintain sleep cycles. This means going to bed at roughly the same time every night and waking at the same time every morning. Trying to sneak extra sleep by hitting snooze on your phone will only serve to make your mind fuzzy and lead to waking up feeling more tired. This extra sleep disrupts your internal clock (Taylor, 2019). When you wake up later than you should, you have returned to a rapid eye movement (REM) cycle where your brain is trying to rest and process subconscious thoughts in dreams. Waking up while in a REM cycle will only serve to make you feel disoriented and foggy.

For optimal sleep, you should try to stick to sleep times, allowing your body to adjust and plan its own sleep cycles. This helps your brain determine when to start a sleep cycle, when to dip into deeper or REM sleep, and when to start waking from this cycle before your morning alarm has even gone off. It's all ordered, and when you mess with it, you mess with your mind.

Tips for Getting a Good Night's Sleep

Oh, we all love a snooze. Certainly, there's nothing quite like it, but is it hitting the sweet spot at bringing you rest? Try these tips to help you maximize rest and minimize stress:

- **Go to Bed Early Enough**

When you stay up late, you will be more tempted to sleep later. This only messes further with your sleep cycles, leaving you more tired and prone to unhappiness.

- **Get Some Movement In**

When you find your sleep is compromised and you suffer symptoms such as restless leg syndrome, chances are that you need to get active. Make sure to get in some stretching or exercising during the day to avoid your body keeping your mind awake.

- **Don't Overstimulate Your Mind**

Most people who suffer from sleep deprivation complain their minds won't switch off. This can be due to them taking stimulants such as caffeine or due to stimulating the brain with activities such as browsing social media, watching TV, or chatting to friends before hitting the sack. Instead, do a routine activity such as meditation or read a calming book to help your brain cycle down, as this will get you to REM sleep much faster.

- **Make a Sleep Cave**

We are still animals at the end of the day, and we need certain conditions to trigger sleep mechanisms in our brains. Darkened rooms free of flashing LED screens and free from droning sounds from machines like aircons or computers will ease your mind and body into natural sleep. Create a sleep cave that is dark, cool, and comfortable. Make sure it is a space you feel safe in as you need your instincts to become calmed too.

- **Lock It Down**

When you are struggling with a brain that just won't switch off as your thoughts keep racing over problems, you can try the following: write down what is bothering you. Think of some possible solutions and write these down too. Both the problem and solutions are now locked down on paper. There is no further need to think this over or mull on the problem. Your mind will start to quiet, and if you find your thoughts turning to the problem, you need only say the words, "It's locked down; there is nothing else I need to think of now." Over time, this will greatly soothe a restless mind, bring you inner quiet, and let you get some quality sleep.

- **Last Resort: Get Medical Help**

You are a physical being, and many of your body processes require a combination of chemicals. It means you need to ensure you get the right chemicals that your body may be deficient in, such as melatonin, which is linked to sleep processes. Your doctor can help you if nothing else succeeds.

There is a proven (and researched) link between good sleep and happiness (Kogan, 2020). While we sleep, we are altering our state of mind from conscious to unconscious thinking. Furthermore, "sleep, by restructuring new memory representations, facilitates extraction of explicit knowledge and insightful behavior" (Ullrich et al., 2004). We can actively process (while sleeping) what we have learned through the day to create a happier mind and a more content life. Make sure to catch up on your Zs, and your happiness will blossom.

Exercise

Recently, a good friend of mine told me they were feeling grumpy and dissatisfied since they hadn't been able to hit the gym during the lockdown. I was a bit astonished about this as I would have counted going to the gym as being less important in the scheme of things. But this got me thinking. How big a role does exercise play in our health and our ability to experience happiness?

Science has discovered exercise is inextricably linked to our ability to function correctly, both mentally and physically. Aerobic exercises stimulate our thinking (Hillman et al., 2008). Exercise improves academic performance, boosts our ability to think creatively and clearly, and improves problem-solving capacities. It directly increases our happiness levels as we can function better. Further studies by Khazaee-Pool (2015) found that in older people, exercise directly correlates to happiness.

There has long been a connection between exercise and an improvement in depression scales. Exercise stimulates thinking, and it increases the production of endorphins or feel-good chemicals that help the brain feel happier. This effect may also help remove negative thinking patterns as you reconnect with your body through exercise.

A depression and aerobic exercise study by Morales et al. (2018) had some interesting findings. Doing regular (instructor-led) aerobic exercise has the benefits of treating major depression with effectiveness similar to conventional antidepressant therapy. Its effect offers a real-world application for mental health services. Not only does aerobic exercise match medical treatments for depression, but it also seems to rival it in its effectiveness. This is great news for those wanting to improve their overall happiness scores as depression is the opposite of being happy.

As little as 10 minutes a day can help (Reynolds, 2018). Climbing the steps instead of taking the elevator, walking downstairs to the park for lunch, or doing some lunchtime yoga can really help get your body and mind in the right place for happiness to be born.

Exercise Considerations for Happiness

When you are planning and performing exercises, there are a few things to think about to maximize your happiness payoff.

- **Focus on How You Feel During and After the Exercise**

Exercise shouldn't be punishment. You should do it because it makes you feel good while you do it and because you see it as an investment in yourself. Doing it because you want to look like someone else will not ensure happiness; however, doing it because you feel excited when you can lift a little more weight or stretch a little further will bring you happiness.

- **Try to Include All Major Exercise Types**

When you start exercising, you should consider what your goals are for doing it. Is it to increase your energy levels or to lose weight so you can move more easily? Whatever your goal, you should try to include various exercise types such as stretching, cardio, weight training, etc. The above studies all confirmed that exercise, especially aerobics, not only improves your health but also stimulates your ability to think, thus improving your mental well-being.

- **Make Exercise Fun**

When exercise is fun, you will enjoy it more, and this will in itself already contribute to your happiness. You will look forward to your daily or weekly gym session or your early morning walks around the park. Adding the element of fun will keep you motivated, and you will gain experience out of it, not simply the benefit of doing. Turning an exercise routine into a treasure hunt or doing it to the beat of your favorite music will help take the "grind" out of exercising.

- **Make an Experience out of It**

If you can turn exercise into a social activity, doing it with some friends, or sharing your goals with people who are fun to be around, you can gain additional happiness currency from the task. You will be looking forward to your exercise routine, and it will help you bust tension, as well as enjoy experiences and memories such as training for a marathon and running with friends. While looking after your body is about exercise, it is also about food, and what you eat, you become. This is more than whether you are trim and lean or fat and flabby.

Food

There is literature available on all sorts of diets, all of them promising amazing results. However, most of them fall short when you actually begin eating cabbage soup three times a day or drink only juiced foods for three weeks. Food is an adversary to many of us.

We all have different body types, and everything about us, from our blood type to our body mass index, contributes to how we interact and react to food. Some of us love food for the sense of satisfaction we get when we eat it, and this often leads to obesity as we chase that thrill of momentarily being satiated.

When you choose a diet that leaves you feeling low in energy and sluggish, your life will mirror it. A diet that causes bloat, indigestion, and constipation will not foster happiness. I learned this quickly, and once I switched to a diet that left me feeling alive and energized, I began to experience happiness manifest in my life more often. For me, this was a plant-based diet, but you may find a diet that suits you better, like the blood type diet, keto diet, or perhaps even becoming a fruitarian. Here, again, I wanted hard facts and to understand how my diet influences my body, so I got educated and certified in the field of vegan sports nutrition and diet plan preparation.

Whatever you eat, you should pay attention to your relationship with food. If you eat because you are feeling unhappy, you are blocking happiness since you have unresolved issues that you are trying to munch through. Likewise, refusing to eat since you want to avoid gaining weight to meet peer approval will also leave you feeling empty.

Considering your overall health, you should follow a food plan that includes all the essential amino acids, macronutrients, and micronutrients you require for optimal health. A deficiency in vitamins can lead to depression, and simply ingesting more natural sources of vitamins or taking a balanced supplement can do wonders for improving your mood and enabling you to experience more happiness.

Happy Gut, Happy Mind

Science is beginning to establish the relationship between the gut and the brain. With good reason, they have taken to calling your gut your second brain.

Gut health improves mental health. Eating a balanced meal is about more than just calories.

The microbiota-gut-brain (MGB) axis has developed to ensure healthy communication and cooperation between the microbiotics in your gut and the resulting processes of these and how they affect your health and the functioning of the brain. It is beneficial to consume foods rich in probiotics as these help to maintain healthy gut health.

The communication process between the brain and the gut involves the endocrine, immune, and neurotransmitters systems, and a "dysfunction of these systems, along with the presence of gut dysbiosis, have been detected among clinically depressed patients" (Yong et al., 2020). Eating probiotic-rich foods help manage depression and other mood disorders, with the bonus of not involving negative side effects of regular pharmacological prescriptions.

The gut microbiome may offer "potential treatments and preventative measures for depressive and anxiety disorders" (Slyepchenko et al., 2014). The probiotics we ingest can offer us ways to improve our health, mental well-being, and boost our happiness. "Pre- and probiotics have shown antidepressant responses and anti-inflammatory effects," which encourage us to add foods containing these to our daily diet (Carlessi et al., 2019).

Our gut microbiome affects not only our digestion, but also our immunity, overall health, and most importantly—our energy levels (Lima-Ojeda et al., 2017). The **probiotics**, or the "good bacteria," that provide all the above-mentioned benefits can be mostly found in:

- **Sauerkraut**

This fermented cabbage is known to contain probiotics and enzymes that improve gut health.

- **Kimchi**

Kimchi is a form of fermented vegetable food, and like Sauerkraut, it contains probiotics, specifically lactic acid bacteria. These again build up your gut biome.

- **Pickled Vegetables**

Fermented or pickled foods contain natural probiotics, and they can help to boost your immune system significantly. Adding a few slices of pickled gherkins can help aid digestion and improve your gut health. Since vinegar can destroy probiotics, it is best to pickle with water and salt.

- **Kombucha**

Likewise, kombucha is made by adding bacteria, yeast, and sugar to different teas, which are then allowed to ferment for one to four weeks. The film that "grows" on top of the tea is rich in probiotics.

- **Kefir**

This plant-based yogurt contains a great variety of bacterial strains and yeasts that are beneficial to your gut health.

- **Tempeh**

Made of fermented soybeans, this product contains a range of bacteria and probiotics that are great for your gut biome.

- **Sourdough Bread**

While baking destroys probiotics and bacteria, this bread retains the lactic acids that still contain the benefits of probiotics. It is also loaded with antioxidants, which help with heart, brain, and gut health.

- **Miso Soup**

This traditional Japanese fermented soup is loaded with probiotics. It protects the gut lining, and since it also contains antioxidants and B vitamins, it is a real winner.

Foods rich in fiber make for excellent sources of prebiotic nutrition that cultivates probiotics; hence, they should form part of your daily meal plan. Prebiotics are the food for probiotic bacteria to feed on. Ingesting it creates a healthy home for the probiotics in your gut. Some good sources of **prebiotics** are:

- **Vegetables:** Cabbage, carrots, and potatoes
- **Fruits and dried fruits:** Apples, pears, and raisins
- **Whole-grain products:** Whole-grain bread or pasta
- **Legumes:** Beans, peas, and lentils
- **Nuts and seeds:** Walnuts, pecan nuts, and peanuts

You should be sure to consume more water as fiber-rich diets can dehydrate your digestive tract and cause constipation. By increasing your water intake, you will ensure that everything flows along nicely.

Planning your diet for probiotic boosting foods doesn't mean you need to eat buckets of sauerkraut or drink gallons of miso soup. Rather, the goal is diversity as each food will contain its unique blend of probiotics depending on how it was processed. So, focus on eating a diverse range of fermented foods to boost your gut health, stimulate your brain, and fuel your happiness.

Eight Happiness Boosting Foods

Additionally to probiotics and prebiotics, research has linked more foods to happiness and significant effects on our moods. These are my favorites that have been proven effective:

- **Black Beans**

Beans are rich in magnesium, and this helps increase serotonin production, which boosts happiness.

- **Whole-Grain Bread**

This complex carbohydrate helps to boost gut health, which directly influences brain health.

- **Beets**

Rich in betaine, beetroots help boost serotonin production and balance hormonal health too.

- **Seaweed**

When your thyroid is on the fizz, happiness can start to disappear from your life. Loaded with iodine, seaweed helps stabilize your thyroid.

- **Berries**

Vitamin C is essential for energy production in your body, and berries are rich in vitamin C. Eating these will help you feel energized. Since they contain resveratrol, they lower depression too.

- **Dark Chocolate**

This yummy food contains cocoa flavonols, which have been proven in research (Nehlig, 2013) to boost cognitive performance. Dark chocolate with a 70% (or more, if you are brave) cocoa content is best for a full nutrient boost. However, more is not "more" in this case, and only a few ounces a day is more than sufficient.

- **Pumpkin Seeds**

These are not just great for the fiber boost, but they are also a great source of tryptophan. Tryptophan is an amino acid that helps with serotonin production, and it can have a calming effect on your general mood. If you feel nibbly at night, these provide a healthy snacking alternative that will calm you before bed.

- **Asparagus**

Another great source of tryptophan is asparagus. It will boost the production of your brain's primary mood-regulating neurotransmitter—serotonin. Since asparagus contains loads of folates, it also helps fight depression.

The list of mood-enhancing foods is quite extensive. As a general guide, I try to eat as widely and diversely as possible, ensuring I get the most out of my meals in terms of vitamins, minerals, amino acids, and other nutrients. I try to get loads of fresh fruits and vegetables, and since I have chosen to follow a plant-based diet, I am very conscious of what I put into my body.

The results have been an improved overall mood, feelings of well-being, and increased energy levels. Whatever diet you choose, make sure to look for more than just weight loss.

If you are supplementing, yet you still feel blue and down, you may need to visit your GP for a blood test to see whether you are missing anything vital. The test will help you determine what you need for optimal health. A healthy body houses a healthy mind, and these are two of the main ingredients for happiness.

How Healthy Are You?

In your journal or book, do the following activities to assess whether your body is a healthy home for a happy mind. These are reflective activities, and you can make changes to your lifestyle based on how you answer. There is no wrong or right answer.

1. *Do you run out of breath quickly?*

Shortness of breath could indicate health problems, lack of fitness, low energy levels, and even borderline depression when your breathing becomes abnormal.

2. *When last did you wake up feeling relaxed and refreshed?*

Keep an eye on your sleep patterns to ensure you get enough rest as this affects your ability to feel energized and happy.

3. *What does your daily meal plan look like?*

Do you eat based on what is readily available, or do you plan balanced meals that help you meet all of your nutritional requirements? Include notes in your journal about how you make efforts to boost the health value of your daily food intake. Track when you eat fresh fruits and vegetables, and when you eat out or opt for fast food. Do you have any negative habits when it comes to your eating? Do you plan your meals not only on what is in the fridge but also on what your body needs?

4. *Are you caring for your body to care for your mind?*

Deciding between caring for your body since it meets a higher purpose or since you are trying to impress someone can be a huge leap into happiness. Self-love is an important factor here. Looking after your body involves self-care, and when you care for your body, you are caring for your mind.

Now evaluate your answers, trying to see where you are falling short, what your targets or areas of focus should be, plan how you will improve your health, and create a body that can house a happy mind.

Chapter 4

Connect with Others

Interdependence is and ought to be as much the ideal of man as self-sufficiency. Man is a social being.

~ Mahatma Gandhi

While happiness is about you, the reality is that you live in the world, and you can and should connect with others. Aristotle, like Gandhi, recognized that we are "social animals," so we should work on this dimension of ourselves and not deny it.

During my travels, I have noticed that people often gravitate towards others, forming lasting bonds, or they avoid relationships, choosing isolation instead. While it may seem wise to rather keep your own company when relationships can be so messy and painful at times, it is not without consequences to choose isolationism.

Simply think of the times you've had to wait in line somewhere. If you managed to strike up a conversation with those around you, time passed much quicker, and the experience was much more pleasurable. However, if you dove into social media instead, you were probably checking the clock and wishing the "ordeal" would be over. Positive experiences can arise from interacting with other people. Choosing only your own company can be less favorable than you'd care to think. Studies proved this theory (Epley and Schroeder, 2014).

Relationships

When we share an experience with others, that experience becomes amplified. If this is a good experience, we enjoy it more, and when this is an unpleasant experience, we feel connected to those sharing it with us. Whether this is a primitive instinct that is left over from our primal days when being in a clan ensured survival or perhaps simply human instinct, we do better when we are connected.

As a baby, you are dependent on others for your care, and this is perhaps where our types of relationship goals form (Wu, 2020). While attachment styles constitute a whole branch of psychology that falls outside of this book's scope, I do want to point out that how we connect to others as a child is how we tend to connect as adults. Our brains have been wired in a certain way, and if you have formed a bad connection framework, it is possible to rewire the brain.

While Abraham Maslow's famous pyramid of needs ranks love and belonging as higher needs, the reality is that we can't exist without them. Your happiness may be created within you, but when you feel alone, isolated, and you don't have any relationships you can count on, you definitely decrease your available resources to create happiness.

When we are in relationships, we experience a need to care, and there is a great pleasure to be found in this. Feeling like we belong, like we matter to someone, is a huge part of our ability to create happiness. While this need not be a significant other or your child, and even if you live alone, having a relationship (which can even be with your six cats) makes us feel like we matter.

Why Do We Need Connection?

German researchers investigated this very question. A 2015 study found that people who connect to other people are happier than those who don't (Newman, 2018). While your happiness isn't solely dependent on making a connection, having some connection definitely improves your chances of being happy.

Connecting to others enriches our experiences of situations, events, and feelings. We make memories with people, and while we can make happy memories with only ourselves in the picture, we do require the sense of belonging that comes from sharing and connecting to others. Research also indicates that doing something with someone can amplify the experience (Boothby, 2014).

Being connected is good for your health, your mental well-being, and your emotional stability. Even if you are an independent person, there are still moments in life when having a person you can turn to for support and care is essential. This is why we have social services in most countries, as responsible governments realize the need for social connection and care. Studies among first-year university students found that those who had social support and connection were less likely to develop depression or flunk out (South University, 2018). Having social connections helps us to persevere when the going gets tough.

Studies among the elderly have concluded that having stable social connections improves your life-expectancy, lowers your risk of dementia and Alzheimer's, and lowers the risk of depression. Meyer (2018a) reported on a host of studies that confirm how being isolated is bad for your health, mental well-being, and emotional vitality. When you have made social connections, you are more likely to turn to others for help and support. They provide you with a support network, and you will have a more positive frame of mind.

Circles Around You

When speaking of social connections, people automatically tend to think of family connections, life partners, or friends; yet, we have a whole range of social circles around us. Within any of these circles, we can build connections. I like to think of this as ripples in a pond. While your immediate circle may be your nuclear family, there are at least a dozen other circles you can connect with to satisfy your social needs.

Examples of happy social connections could include:

Lisa lives alone, and she takes great joy in walking her two dogs every day at the park, where she greets other regular faces. She shares a few words with the ice cream vendor when she buys a cone on Sunday afternoons, and she frequently chats to the dog walkers who frequent the park.

While her connections may not be intimate, they are a part of her life, and they make her belong, giving routine and happiness to her life.

Bob is a regular guy, and while he holds a fairly low paying job, he has three beautiful children and a loving wife he dotes on.

He is able to carry on, even when he is unhappy at his job, as he has the support of his family.

Sam is an orphan, and he lives in a crowded foster home. Yet, he is happy as he has the company of 10 other boys who share their lives and experiences with him.

In this instance, Sam is able to create happiness as he isn't alone in his trials. He can connect and relate to the other boys. Because he doesn't suffer alone, he finds the strength to carry on.

Any social connection can serve to help you create happiness. Even if you have no friends and feel socially awkward, you can find a connection in a pet or a casual conversation with someone who moves in your circles. Taking on charity work when you are isolated is an excellent way to reach out and connect with others. It's hard to feel alone and depressed while serving soup at a local shelter and seeing the gratitude and happy smiles that such a simple token can bring to others. Connection, even with strangers, is essential. It grounds you, helps you, and empowers you.

While you can't choose family, and there are some of us who are cursed with terrible family members, we can choose friends, and we can interact with strangers. Any connection creates positive energy and forward momentum in your life. I remember going for my first job interview and telling the taxi driver that I was nervous. He kindly cheered me on, encouraging me, and as a result, I was so optimistic when I went in for the interview that I aced it right away. The smallest connection can have huge ripple effects, leading you to achievements and happiness you never knew possible.

Social connections and goals are also easier to achieve than personal or material goals. Through them, you can experience satisfaction and enjoyment more frequently. Calling up a friend can more easily make you feel good than trying to lose 20 pounds does. While you need social and personal goals to achieve real happiness, having good social connections can help you maintain daily contentment. This, in turn, helps create the energy to help you strive for more difficult happiness goals that are personal and only involve you.

Solitude Versus Connection Dynamics

Studies have found that people enjoy the opportunity to open up and really share their personal feelings, experiences, and thoughts, and that there is a link to increased well-being in doing so. This might also be why psychologists are so popular. However, the closer and more trusting the connection, the more gratifying the experience (Sun et al., 2019). When people feel like they can confide in someone they know, there is a much deeper sense of satisfaction and lasting happiness.

Sharing victories helps you double the enjoyment, and asking for help and receiving it helps generate feelings of goodwill. Asking for help makes us human, and we often receive support from the most unlikely people. This element of surprise can create happiness in itself. Pursuing a life of solitude would have completely stopped any chance of this help being there for you. While most of us have stories of our trust being broken by a friend or partner, we do need to reach out to manage our social goals. In turn, this has the wonderful result of restoring our trust and renewing hope. Both—hope and trust are powerful forces for positive energy and happiness.

Paradoxically, it has been proven (Epley & Schreuder, 2014) that we expect to be more satisfied and happy if we keep a distance from strangers and don't engage in conversations with them, but the opposite is true. While isolation may seem more positive, there is a cost. Sharing experiences, even with strangers, can be hugely beneficial. It can help manage fear, depression, and anxiety. Simply talking to someone can help to lessen your emotional load. Just think of the times you've spoken to someone while in an unpleasant situation (like waiting in line or sitting outside the dentist's office) and felt the situation improve.

When trying to achieve happiness, a self-focused approach is unlikely to succeed. Yes, you create your happiness, but when you are only focused on yourself, you will tend to become decidedly unhappy. Being unable to share happy feelings will diminish them. People who tend to only look inward often seek happiness in material things, and they lack the experience of real happiness. As our discussion in Chapter 2 indicated, spending money on things and not on experiences is not the way to reach happiness. Isolating yourself will achieve the same result, as you are spending your energy and time only on yourself, meaning you are focused on things and not on experiences (with neither other people nor other living beings).

Recognizing the interdependence we have on each other is the beginning of belonging, acceptance, and social happiness. While being a strong individual is also part of achieving your happiness, only seeing yourself and your needs will blind you to the world and the people you live among.

Hand in hand with this is the negative penchant of most people to complain endlessly. This negative pattern of thinking is sure to ruin any chance of you creating happiness. Whether you are the person who talks negatively or complains, or someone else is the complainer, negativity breeds negativity. Make sure the circles around you are filled with people who talk about good things—like their hopes, dreams, happiness, gratitude, and positivity. If you tend to be negative, surrounding yourself with people like this will help you focus on the positive and lift you out of the risk of developing depression that comes with negative talk.

There is a notable tendency of people to become embedded in the social networks that they function in. When something then happens to one person, the whole group suffers for it. Examples of this would include a group member passing away and leaving the group in mourning.

"Emotional states can be transferred directly from one individual to another by mimicry and 'emotional contagion'" (Hatfield et al., 1993). We adopt the emotional expressions of the people around us. So, if we surround ourselves with negative people, we will become "contaminated" by that same negativity through proximity. Studies where university students were assigned a depressive roommate, soon had test subjects showing signs of depression themselves (Howes et al., 1985).

Gravitate towards positive people for your social connections. If your regular taxi driver moans non-stop about their ugly mother-in-law, then choose to take the bus instead. Should you end up next to a stranger who is clearly on a venting binge, politely move to a different seat. If you can't move away from the negative talker, try to steer the conversation towards positive topics or share some of your happiness. Don't get dragged down by other people's drama.

While I've already indicated that choosing to be alone most of the time is not healthy, nor does it lead to contentment, being lonely can be forced on you by circumstances. What you do about this will influence not only your health but also your happiness.

The American Association of Retired Persons (AARP) conducted a study that found 35% of older people are lonely (Meyer, 2018b). The first step to banishing loneliness is to be aware of your community involvement. While your family may disappoint you, reaching out to wider circles can help you make a connection.

When you know you are not pulling your social weight, you can begin to reach out and make connections. The goal here is not to suddenly become a Facebook sensation; instead, your goal is to make real human contact. Being able to reach out and touch or hug someone is a great way to help bring meaning and purpose into your life. When you have found some purpose, you will experience happiness blossoming.

Reciprocity Effect

When you reach out to others, you achieve more. The concept of reciprocity means you give to others, and they are then more likely to give to you. This exchange of energy, effort, and contact helps foster connection and resilience.

By helping others, we, in turn, get help. It enables us to do things we can't do alone. With the additional help, we are given more resources and discover more resourcefulness in ourselves. These all make for better preparedness and effectiveness in creating a happy life.

How Connected Are You?

Sometimes we are more connected than we know, and simply being aware of our connections can be a great confidence booster. I am not talking about the 3,500 Facebook friends you have (although some of them may be genuine friends). Instead, I am referring here to the people in your life, whether they are tiny ripples in your connection pond or huge waves, who connect with you in some way.

In your journal, write down a list of the people you interact with regularly. You can include anyone you see more than just once. Your list might consist of the bus driver, your doorman, the florist on the corner, the assistant at the coffee shop you frequent every morning, the receptionist at work, a colleague, your priest, and whomever else. The list can go on and on.

Now give each person on that list a rating out of five based on how good they make you feel after you have interacted with them. It doesn't matter if that interaction is only a few seconds or a 10-minute chat every morning. Reflect on what feeling they motivate in you.

The doorman who asks if you are well, tells you to have a splendid day, opens the door, carries some groceries to the elevator for you when you're overloaded after shopping, might get a score of $\frac{4}{5}$. The grumpy bus driver might not get a good score since you leave his bus in the morning feeling blue.

Here's the fun part. Using a whole page, draw a bucket shape (it doesn't have to be fancy). In this bucket, list all the people you interact with daily who have scored $\frac{3}{5}$ and above. These are your connections. Your real connections. How full is your bucket? Did you expect this much support in your bucket?

Now that you are aware of how you are being supported, you can link this up with the generosity effect that you read about in Chapter 2. Plan to do something small for these people to show your gratitude. You don't have to say anything, and chances are that they will not understand how they contribute to your life or happiness. However, as you see their joy at a small token like giving your doorman a tip, leaving some freshly baked cookies for the taxi driver, or making sure to buy flowers every week from the florist can help your happiness grow as you relish your connection to them.

Chapter 5

Acts of Kindness

No act of kindness, no matter how small, is ever wasted.

~ Aesop

Human kindness is one of the strongest forces in the world. It has the power to move nations and end wars. It can even change the way you see yourself and your life. When you think of kindness, remember that it starts with you.

Most of us want to receive kindness, and when we experience some rough going, we are quick to think the world is a cruel place, forgetting that we are a part of that world. The first act of kindness should then be to yourself by yourself. No effort on yourself is ever wasted.

Your Blessings: Kindness and Forgiveness

The roots of kindness can be found in self-love and self-care. Meeting your physical, emotional, and mental needs is what self-love is all about. When you take care of your needs, you are busy creating a body, mind, and spirit that are happy. At the same time, you are creating inner happiness, and you are able to freely give kindness to others. I would remind you of the generosity effect that we covered in Chapter 2. When you can give money or spend energy on someone, you feel the glow of that connection too.

Kindness is about more than just taking a long bath after a difficult day or any other self-care activity. Self-care activities like journaling, lighting some candles, going on a meditation retreat, or taking a weekend break are all examples of kindness. Still, they are not the full extent of kindness. You see, kindness is also a mindset where you show yourself compassion and learn to take it just a little easier on yourself.

Showing yourself kindness is about becoming your own friend, and it is about being your own best supporter. This helps to create a happy mind. It helps you stay motivated to carry on when you are facing difficult odds.

There is a relationship between having the personal quality of kindness and developing happiness in your life. Proving this theory was done with a simple test where participants had to count their acts of kindness (to themselves and others) for a week. When the study's participants reflected on how many times they had shown kindness, their happiness levels increased simply by realizing they were kind. This study also found that happy people were more motivated to perform, and they were more likely to show gratitude to those who helped them, thereby further increasing their happiness. Kindness (and gratitude), therefore, produce subjective happiness (Otake et al., 2006).

So, why are more people not kind to themselves? Surely, showing yourself kindness is satisfying, and it makes you happy, so what's there to lose by practicing self-care and kindness? It is not as simple as just loving yourself or taking care of yourself—there is the matter of forgiveness.

Our societal view of people and ourselves often circles on the belief that we have somehow transgressed or sinned, and as a result, we need to be punished. You may have been preconditioned into a guilt complex (Good Therapy, n.d.). Whether this is due to society, culture, religion, or socializing errors, we end up with a mountain of self-inflicted guilt. Your thinking patterns often mirror negative self-views, and you begin to believe you need to be punished. This drains your happiness and demotivates you from making changes that could improve your life.

Perhaps you secretly see yourself as sinful since you are living with a boyfriend before marriage, or you think you somehow shamed your parents. The list of subconsciously perceived transgressions could contain massive booboos or even little slip-ups. The result is the same—a guilt complex. Introspection will help you decide whether you "deserve" to be happy or not.

Self-love is about healing your life, your thinking, and changing your actions resulting from previous negative self-views. Whatever you find during introspection, you don't deserve punishment. To really enjoy your life, you need to forgive yourself and practice self-love and self-compassion. These lead to self-forgiveness, and this is where real happiness can begin to change your life.

Until you forgive yourself for whatever you think you have done to deserve punishment, you will not be able to create real and abundant happiness. This was a powerful realization to me, and once I began to delve through my memories and found the years-forgotten trauma that had convinced me I didn't deserve to be happy, I could finally forgive myself and create happiness again.

Now, I wouldn't have been able to get to the point of forgiveness without first undoing some self-inflicted damage with acts of kindness. These acts of kindness were not about suddenly loving myself and dressing pretty and going out with friends. Instead, it was a range of small actions to take care of my needs. In the beginning, I felt like I was faking it, and this is where science saved me.

I looked at the Otake study into acts of kindness, and I tried it for myself. For a whole week, I engaged in random acts of kindness. These were not pre-planned or for specific people. They were really simple acts of "paying it forward." With each action, whether it was giving the bus driver a packet of cookies or donating old clothes to the homeless man who begs down the road from my office building, I could feel my happiness meter climb.

Soon, I was excited to do something for someone else, and I began doing things for myself too. I was motivated. Kindness had created motivation, and happiness was short on its heels.

When you perform acts of kindness for yourself, you want to share it. A person you were kind to might do something kind for the next person. Kindness—as many studies have proven—is contagious (Le Roy, 2016).

Sharing Kindness with Others

Kindness is made to be shared. It creates an afterglow when you perform an act of kindness for someone. Whether you are kind to yourself or to a complete stranger, it doesn't matter—the effects are the same.

Multiple theories on different kinds of altruism predict "that people will be happy to help family, friends, community members, spouses, and even strangers under some conditions." (Curry et al., 2018). This motivation to help makes us happy. We are happy because we feel like a situation is in the process of being solved, and our world feels ordered again. Therefore, sharing kindness directly translates into feelings of happiness.

Studies have also found that when the number of kindness acts increases, the feeling of happiness increases proportionately (Rowland & Curry, 2019). These feelings of bliss that result from an act of kindness may trigger a range of emotional responses. There are benefits to acting kindly, whether to yourself, your immediate group (including friends and family), and others (distant familiar people and complete strangers).

Benefits of Acts of Kindness

Kindness can bring real relief and happiness if you use it wisely.

- **Giving kindness causes feelings of love**

When people are on the receiving end of kindness, they feel loved. Someone noticed them, and this makes them feel valued. Love is not a one-way street, so giving love to someone else makes us feel loved too.

- **Both parties involved in the act of kindness feel awe**

We love watching videos or reading stories of random acts of kindness. There is something about these that fill us with awe and that feel-good glow. Awe is inspiring, and when we can receive kindness or give it and trigger that feeling, we imagine a life with possibilities instead of limitations. Happiness follows when we don't feel limited, and awe frees us from negative life views (even if only for a moment).

- **You feel invigorated by acting kindly**

Have you ever been excited about doing something nice for someone? Perhaps you have planned it, and you lie awake the night before, anticipating their reaction and imagining how much the person will like your token or act of kindness. Your excitement is an indication of how invigorated you feel. Anticipation and the gratitude of the recipient of the kindness act are powerfully invigorating forces.

- **Your self-worth increases**

When people thank you, your natural instinct is to feel valued. This, in turn, enhances your sense of self-worth. Knowing that you can do things for others that make them happy can create happiness in your mind.

- **Kindness has chemical effects**

Since giving and doing for someone else creates feelings of being loved, your body produces the hormone oxytocin and the neurotransmitters—serotonin and endorphin. These have the effects of increasing self-esteem and optimism, and they improve blood pressure and reduce stress. Endorphins also fight feelings of pain.

Kindness lowers cortisol (the stress hormone) by 23% (Stoerkel, 2020). This means doing nice things for others and for yourself will lower your stress levels significantly. In essence, kindness is beneficial for you. It makes you stress less, feel better, and it boosts your self-esteem, as well as creates happiness.

Kindness has a measurable effect on those who witness it. In a 2015 study, researchers coined the term “moral elevation” to describe the heightened emotional state that people reach when they witness an act of kindness. The study participants reported elevated heart rates and increased brain activity when they watched videos showing acts of kindness. Prosocial activity, such as kindness, is then linked to a significant physiological response (Le Roy, 2016). It might explain why we react emotionally when we see this type of behavior in a movie or real life. We feel the gift of that kindness, even when it isn’t directed at us.

The Ripple Effect

Is kindness merely a once-off transaction or exchange? Science has argued that kindness echoes out based on proximity (like a contagion). This is known as the ripple effect, and it is measured in terms of how many people benefit through happiness from an original act of kindness.

In reality, it might look something like this:

A man gets a sudden windfall through an unexpected raise in pay at his job, which his boss kindly awarded him in recognition of his years of service. He is happy, and as a result, he shows kindness to his family, and he takes them away for a weekend getaway. By extension, his family is now happy too. While their happiness may not be as large as the man's, the effect still continues. The man's family further invites their friends to get together for a barbeque. They are happy with the social experience, and the initial happiness ripples out, diffusing among the (invited) people who are affected. While these people had nothing to do with the initial act of kindness, they now feel happy too.

Hence, happiness can be shared. Acts of kindness lead to happiness, and since we can and do share our experience of kindness, we do also share happiness.

A simple example of sharing with strangers might include the man in the scenario above, giving a vendor selling hotdogs a huge tip when he buys lunch on the day he received the raise.

Like ripples in a pond, the ripples of kindness move out from the initial kindness receiver, and those who are affected, in turn, affect others. Kindness (and the happiness it creates) can then spread like a virus! The implications of this for a better world are immense.

How Kind Are You?

Like the kindness experiments listed in this chapter, it is time to see how kind you are. This is not about self-praise or getting a big head. Instead, you are going to realize the power you have to change the world (and yourself too).

1. In your journal, write down all the acts of kindness you have performed every day for the last week. These acts can be large, medium, or small. Be sure to write down how you felt while you were doing these, how the recipient of the kindness reacted, and perhaps (if you know) whether the kindness rippled out to someone else. It might look something like this:

Monday

- Opened the door for an elderly lady entering my office building. She smiled at me, and I felt good for being able to help.
- Shared a pizza I bought for lunch with a colleague. We enjoyed a good chat while we ate, and later I saw him hand his lunch (which he had brought from home) to a homeless man, who smiled in surprise (ripple effect).
- Walking home, I helped a florist carry his buckets of flowers inside before the afternoon rainstorm hit. He was very grateful and gave me a bouquet of flowers to brighten my home. We both felt happy as he didn't lose money on spoiled flowers (from the storm), and I got to take lovely flowers (and his smile) home.

2. Now, once you have written down the acts of kindness for the day, give yourself exactly 60 seconds to write down all that went wrong this day. Notice that the bigger your list of kindness acts is, the shorter your list of complaints becomes. When you feel the

afterglow of giving and doing nice things for others, you don't see the negatives. What may have felt like the end of the world when it happened during your day loses its power over you. You are wrapped in the positivity of your kindness, and you gain a perspective in life that fosters happiness daily.

3. Install a kindness app on your phone. If you are struggling with doing acts of kindness for the people you meet, you can use an app for this purpose. Such an app can generate ideas on how to practice acts of random kindness. It offers daily suggestions to help you think of creative and novel ways to be kind to others and yourself. Alternatively, you could create a kindness jar in which you place kindness ideas written on slips of paper. Every day you can draw one idea and see if you can perform the act of kindness this day. Ideas could include picking up trash on your morning walk, smiling at five strangers, or packing an extra lunch for a colleague. Don't forget to write about the experience in your journal, as this helps train your brain to seek (and see) happiness.

Chapter 6

The Magic of Gratitude

Reflect upon your present blessings—of which every man has many—not on your past misfortunes, of which all men have some.

~ Charles Dickens

Gratitude is something most of us know we should practice, yet we often get caught up in drama and unnecessary things that damage our calm. I was reminded of this the other day when I met with a friend for coffee. She had just come from a morning of shopping and paying bills, and I could see she was flustered. As soon as she sat down, before our menus had even arrived while at the coffee shop, she began verbal vomiting.

You know that feeling when someone's emotions and anxiety hit you in the face before their words even do? Yip; this was just such an occasion. I listened patiently as she told me all about her "terrible" morning. She described in great detail how "dreadful" traffic had been and how she had "almost" dinged her brand new Mercedes. Her description included how she had struggled to find the right size at the upscale boutique where she was shopping. The assistants had tried to help, but ultimately, she couldn't find what she was looking for.

After she finally ran out of words and began sipping her coffee, which she complained was too hot, I decided to say something (my first words in about 15 minutes). I asked her what about her day had been irreparable.

She looked at me in confusion. Then she became a bit defensive. How could I ask her that? After all, she had just had the worst day, or had she?

You see, where she had chosen the negative to focus on, I could see loads of things she could instead have been grateful for. For starters, she could afford to drive a fancy car (gratitude number 1), and while traffic was heavy, and she had almost banged her car—she hadn't, and her car was scratch free (gratitude number 2). While she didn't find her ideal size at the boutique, this was also a blessing in disguise as she really didn't need more clothes (gratitude number 3). The shop assistants had been friendly, and they had tried to help her (gratitude number 4), so I couldn't see anything that had gone wrong with her day at all.

As I explained this to her, my friend looked at me in slack-jawed amazement. Then, she became quiet, and I could see my words sink home. You see, gratitude is a light that shines in the dark and lets us see what is real and what is not.

I am not overly religious, but the Bible has it right when it says, "Count your blessings." As a bonus, when you do count your blessings, they multiply as a result. Blessings are nothing else except things, events, and situations we should be grateful for. It is a life perspective that has the power to change negative thoughts to positive ones. It energizes, and it gives you forward momentum (just like kindness).

Hi, My Name Is Gratitude

I have come to think of gratitude as my friend, who leads me to happiness. When friends ask me about my journey into happiness, I often tell them about gratitude, and I introduce it like a friend. You could almost say, "Hi, my name is Gratitude, and I love ..."

But always, I turn back to the science of things as I don't do hocus pocus or mindless philosophies. If science backs it, then so do I, and it hasn't led me astray so far.

You see, gratitude is a powerful force in your life, and when you start practicing it, you will begin to experience a whole load of physical changes. This is what science has shown to be true:

Hanson (2011) reports on the interaction between our thoughts and our brain. He finds that the more you think negative thoughts, the more you increase the production of the hormone cortisol in the brain, which destroys the hippocampus (our emotion center). Conversely, when you practice mindfulness, think happy thoughts, and are generally positively (and gratefully) minded, your left prefrontal cortex will be more developed. This part of the brain is designed to help manage stressful thoughts and avoid overthinking, thereby reducing the production of cortisol.

You may have noticed that you become more forgetful when you are stressed, and in extreme cases, you may forget something entirely. This is because of the damage caused by cortisol to the memory centers of your brain (Hanson, 2011). Hence, cutting down on cortisol production should be a priority if you want to be healthy, maintain mental health, and live a happy life.

Gratitude, my dearest friend on the road to happiness, has many powers, and one of them is that it makes your brain feel good. When you are practicing gratitude daily, you will experience a marked reduction in cortisol production.

"Research suggests that when people practice gratitude, they experience a general alerting and brightening of the mind, and that's probably correlated with more of the neurotransmitter norepinephrine" (Hanson, 2011). This neurotransmitter is known to increase alertness. It is often prescribed as a mood enhancer along with other serotonin-norepinephrine reuptake inhibitors (SNRIs), which stop your brain from breaking down norepinephrine and serotonin. This helps your brain to have more of these chemicals at hand to boost your happiness (Purse, 2020).

Additionally, having a better mood and being more positive also creates better overall health, boosts your immune system, and lowers blood pressure since you will stress less. Gratitude is then really the proverbial friend you can turn to when you need to vent. Like I did on my coffee date with my negatively minded friend, gratitude can help you see things in perspective. When your mind wants to make a mountain out of a molehill, you can use gratitude to bring you back on track as you count your blessings.

Journeys into Gratitude

Learning to know what gratitude is can be approached like a journey with a new friend. You need to do fun things together to build up your communication. There will be awkward moments in the beginning, but you simply need to keep talking to each other, and you will also begin to enjoy the benefits of having gratitude in your life.

One of the ways in which you can get to know your gratitude is to take up gratitude journaling. Whether you write in a book or use an online app that helps you journal, you will be getting to know gratitude. Writing down what you can be grateful for in your daily life (big and small) in your journal will give you ways to reflect on your blessings.

It is easy to latch onto negative experiences, but these are transient. There is always a silver lining, and writing down and talking about it helps to build happiness. Research has shown that when you focus (by writing) on an experience, your gratitude increases greatly (Walker et al., 2016). Keeping a gratitude journal for eight weeks has also been proven in scientific studies to reduce inflammation in those with heart conditions while improving their overall mood and health (Allen, 2018).

Other gratitude awareness activities include writing a letter expressing your gratitude to someone. Researchers tracked this afterglow of happiness that comes from quantifying your happiness on paper and found the effect to last as much as three months after delivering the letter (Brown & Wong, 2017). Ideally, you should deliver this letter in person to the recipient, watching their expression as they read the message. You will instantly respond to this, mirroring their joy and contentment. Perhaps this is why birthday or gift cards are so popular as you are given an opportunity to express your feelings of gratitude for someone who matters to you.

Letter writing is a particularly revealing activity as it makes you aware of your misconceptions regarding gratitude. We often believe that our expression of gratitude doesn't mean much to others, and we might even think that there will be awkwardness when we express gratitude in public. However, seeing that people really appreciate it when we show our gratitude to them can be heartwarming and good for your sense of happiness. Those receiving the gratitude usually also find happiness in it, and this, in turn, is likely to stimulate your contentment. This sharing creates bonds and further builds avenues to experience happiness from having friendship and companionship.

Discovering Gratitude

Gratitude is something many people take for granted. We already assume we have gratitude, or we imagine we don't have to use it since we don't trust the intentions of those we should show gratitude to. Neuroticism can certainly lead to us living without gratitude as we see every situation as coming with strings attached, and therefore, we think we don't have to be grateful.

The reality is—we don't always value that which we should be grateful for. While we can focus on the things we should be thankful for, this often does not have the desired effect of making people value what they have. Instead, imagining the things that bring you gratitude never happened at all makes us aware of how much we rely on someone or something. What if the things you should be grateful for are suddenly "subtracted" (Koo, 2008) from your life? When you begin to think of your life in terms of the things you take for granted as being absent, you realize how big a role they play in your life, which increases your life satisfaction.

Imagine if your wife had suddenly never existed at all. What if your husband never existed, or your job had never been there? While your initial reaction may be to have a nervous little giggle, you will soon begin to realize that the absence of something does indeed make the heart grow fonder. When participants in the study wrote about their life as if their partner had never been part of that life, they were happier with their partner and their life as a result. Writing about their romantic partner did not produce the same feelings of happiness as writing about not meeting that person. Oddly, in a study conducted into this mental subtraction of a positive event from their lives, researchers found that respondents reported improved mood and feelings of well-being when they wrote about this missing event as if it was a surprise to them that it had happened. Writing about how something had happened didn't produce positive writing or emotional reactions in participants (Koo et al., 2008).

Perhaps you have discovered things to be grateful for, and chances are that you will thank people every day you can (or remember to), and you might write in your journal about gratitude. You may even have every conviction to do so every day for the rest of your life. But ... Well, we humans quickly tire of something, especially when the novelty wears off. So, how do you keep gratitude alive?

While you may have created a mindset that looks for gratitude, you will quickly fall into the pattern where "thank you" becomes a vestigial expression. It loses meaning fast, and you may regress to only saying it because it's polite.

Real gratitude demands work. Every day, look for new and novel things to be grateful for. Use it as a way to bring wonder into your life. Be grateful for the experience of the first spring rain that changes the park into an olfactory kaleidoscope. Notice how the streets are clean every morning as you get up. Perhaps rise even earlier to see the patterns around your neighborhood that you don't normally notice. You might be grateful for the fresh bagels you buy for breakfast when you see the bakers arrive at the bakery at four a.m. to start kneading dough or take delivery of huge bags of flour.

Everything around you can hold wonder if you look with the eyes of gratitude at them. Carpenter (2020) recommends seeing details and not large scales when looking at the people, places, and experiences in your life you should be grateful for. Simply writing that your husband is amazing in your journal every night might get old very quickly. However, writing about how he helps you blow out your hair or how he massages your feet while you catch up on paperwork will certainly keep your thanks fresh!

The Comparison Guide

Gratitude is something we feel for what we have, not for what we don't have. It is, however, often determined by comparisons. You might feel gratitude for your older model car when you look at your neighbor whose car is falling apart. Your gratitude would be for your car that is at least in running condition.

By comparing something we have to what others have, we are creating a reference point. It may look like, "I am grateful that my car is better than Tom's car, but Bob across the street has a new Mercedes, so my car isn't that hot either." In this comparison, you have created a reference system that is based on negatives. Negative comparisons or reference points don't bring real gratitude. Instead, these reference points can create a feeling of lack.

Comparisons or reference points should be about you and not about other people. When you compare yourself to yourself, there is no room for envy or jealousy. Instead, you compete *with* yourself, not *against* others. You may create a reference point of your old job, where you may have been miserable. When you compare it to your new job, you feel incredibly grateful for your job as it is better than your old job. If you were to compare your job to your friend's job, you would create either envy or snobbery, neither of which is beneficial to your gratitude development.

Reference points are like road markers in your life. You can create them on the road ahead of you (I've always wanted to finish my degree), you can place them behind you (I don't ever want to be without an education again), or you can place them right where you are (I am so blessed that I'm able to attend the classes and keep learning).

Using these reference points, you can track your achievements, and you can see who or what brought you to where you are. This gives you concrete ways to be grateful. It keeps envy at bay as you can't be focused on *your* reference points and be jealous of others at the same time.

When creating comparisons, be sure to use reference points that are about you compared to yourself and not you compared to others. The idea is to develop gratitude, which builds happiness, not to create jealousy that leads to life dissatisfaction.

The Generosity and Ripple Effect

Just like kindness ripples out, generosity has a similar communal effect. Studies have shown that gratitude, when expressed, encourages positive social action or generosity from the recipients (Grant & Gino, 2010). In the study, participants were generously thanked for their contribution to a project. In turn, the recipients of the gratitude expression were motivated to effect a prosocial activity such as doing charity work or giving to strangers. This was attributed to recipient's feelings, such as a boost in self-worth—they were motivated to act prosocially since they felt socially valued.

We like to be thanked. It makes us feel like we have achieved something, like we are good enough, and once we feel like this, we tend to reach out to others to share that through prosocial efforts. Similar behavior can be seen with animals, who are more likely to groom others when they have been groomed themselves or when they have enjoyed rewards or praise from their caregivers. Prosocial behavior is not limited to humans. It is a survival mechanism, and the generosity effect is designed to share goodwill between the members of the society, herd, or group.

Do You Practice Gratitude?

While you are already journaling, which is one of the top gratitude activities, there is also a range of other activities you can consider diving into. Develop your gratitude muscles and get your mind ready for blessings. These **gratitude activities** will help you create a better reference frame (yours and not your neighbor's).

- **Gratitude Pebbles**

This is a great way to remind yourself to practice gratitude. You can collect some random river stones that are nice and flat and small enough to fit in your pocket. Make a daily habit of choosing a new rock to carry and touch every day. Using a marker, write what you want to feel grateful for on it. Some examples could include "My folks are still alive," or "Today, I woke up in time for sunrise," or "My friend is meeting me for coffee at lunchtime."

These gratitude pebbles make an innovative gift too, if you feel inclined to share your progress on the happiness journey with a loved one. You could place a collection of stones in a jar with some tinsel and a marker with one stone done as an example: "I am grateful for this dear friend."

- **Powerful Prompts**

You can use a gratefulness app, which sends you daily prompts to help you discover what you are grateful about, or you can make your own powerful prompt pot. Essentially, this is a pot into which you put different prompts to help you journal or reflect. Simply write some prompts on slips of paper every time you have a moment and chuck them into your power pot. This works a little like the gratitude jar I discussed earlier. You draw out a daily prompt to help you reflect. Prompts could be like these examples, but be brave and make up your own:

- Today, I am grateful for the first three things I saw.
- Right now, I am grateful for this person, who did ...
- At this moment, I am grateful for feeling ...

- **Twenty-Second Gratitude Grab**

This activity may seem strange, but imagine your house is on fire. You have 20 seconds to grab what matters most to you. It can be people, items, or memories (that you made in your house). Now sit quietly, and for each item, person, or memory you recalled that you grabbed, write two sentences explaining why you are grateful for each of them.

The goal here is to remind you of what you have, what you have created, and who you share your space and life with. In writing about each, you are explaining to your brain why you are grateful, and you build your happiness when you realize you are truly blessed.

Okay, so what do you do when you look around your room or house, and there's nothing you want to grab? Some of us have lives that are not on track to achieving our happiness goals, but this doesn't mean you "burn" with your house. Instead, you may simply have to start with basic things or think harder. When you think hard enough, you will find something that you are grateful for.

You can also use this as an opportunity to think about what is missing from your life that you would be grateful to have. Whatever you come up with needs to really add happiness to your life, not status. You might list something like a partner, a pet, photo albums of wonderful places I wanted to visit, or letters from people I have met all over the world.

- **New Year's Jar**

When you get to New Year's, you are likely to have a whole list of things you want to lose or change. You want to lose weight, change jobs, or lose the things in your life you no longer like.

This activity in gratitude takes up to 365 days. Yip, it's a year-long commitment. You will need a large glass jar, slips of paper, and a colorful set of markers. Throughout the next year, you will be using your keen powers of observation in your life. Write down all the amazing things that happen or that you experience for which you are grateful. You should add details as you might not remember why the sunset was so beautiful on a specific day. You can add to that slip that you were grateful since you had just put your dog to sleep the previous afternoon to end their suffering, and you spent the whole night crying, but in the morning, you were soothed by the beautiful sunrise. You felt that your dog had gone to doggy heaven, and your grief lessened, for which you were grateful.

You will see the things you are grateful for start to fill up the jar (and your life), and it makes you mindful of looking for more to add. When the next New Year's rolls around, make a ritual out of opening the jar, taking out the slips of paper, and briefly reminiscing about each gratitude. The coming year will start with a positive bang, and you will feel inspired to look at life with the eyes of appreciation.

Throughout your journey into the factors that affect happiness, you have been circling closer to your inner self. Happiness is, after all, created inside yourself.

While you have thus far learned about kindness and gratitude and how these can help shift your mind from negative thoughts to a happiness mentality, you need to be living in the present moment to fully experience contentment.

Chapter 7

Be Present

Do not dwell in the past, do not dream of the future, concentrate the mind on the present moment.

~ Buddha

Being present is not something that refers to walking into a room or showing up to work, although you may very well be present at these moments. Instead, being present describes your mental focus at this moment. Focusing your concentration is about connecting with this moment, this place, your body, your mind, and the person or presence you are with.

When you actively bond with yourself, you allow your focus to deepen on what is happening and what you are feeling and thinking right now. This way, you will experience the "now" much more intensely than when you are living in your head or rushing from point A to B.

Interestingly, Killingsworth (2013) found that a staggering 47% of all participants in his study were engaged in daily mind-wandering. It means they were busy thinking about something other than what they were doing or experiencing at that moment. This study also revealed that when our minds are wandering off, we are less happy. Our minds are distracted, and whether we are engaging in mind-wandering to escape an unpleasant experience or doing so simply out of habit, the reality is that we are living outside of our realities when we are not fully engaged with this moment.

For sure, there is a load of people who spend most of their lives wishing they were somewhere else. They are stuck in the clouds that fill their heads. This is different from having a dream that you work towards. Instead, these people simply fantasize, but they make nothing of it, and therefore, they can't get any enjoyment from their dreams. Mind-wandering will not bring happiness, and it will not improve the quality of your life (Killingsworth, 2013).

This study by Killingsworth also found that people tend to lack focus and engage in mind-wandering in almost all activities they were engaged in. From 65% while showering, 50% while working to the lowest 10% while having sex, people tend to be thinking of things other than what they are busy with. It almost appears to be ubiquitous, with people seeming to have no control over how and when their minds wander. The question is then what the cost of this mind-wandering is to their perception and enjoyment of their present moment.

As a paradox, the study also found that people are not happy when their minds are wandering. While we don't always enjoy an activity (especially a boring one like brushing our teeth), we are happier when we focus on that activity than when we do the activity while our minds wander. Clearly, having a wandering mind leads to a state of mental vagueness and uncertainty that the mind doesn't enjoy. In fact, mind-wandering is not a result of unhappiness, but it can cause it. When you are focused on what you are doing (even when it's not something you like doing), you are happier, and the task will likely be completed with greater efficiency.

I Wonder ...

Being stuck on a cloud, dreaming of being happy is what many people experience every day. Just look at the blank faces you see at work. You may be speaking to someone, but their faces have glazed over like cupcake frosting melting off a tasty treat. Except, there's nothing tasty about seeing that vacant look in their eyes. It is not a look of joy, and there is a total lack of energy in these people. Perhaps you are even one of the frosting people?

Wondering about a better life isn't the same as doing something about improving the quality of your life. Now, I am not saying you need to do anything drastic, but you may need to engage in some self-examination and introspection to see what it is about your current life that has you chasing clouds instead of living it. Why are you avoiding this moment? What should you be doing at this moment?

Csikszentmihalyi (1990) theorized that the mind is usually chaotic, and if we don't learn to gain control over our thoughts, they will spiral down to random patterned thinking that usually lingers on painful or negative thoughts and memories. Just think about what happens to your mind when you are trying (unsuccessfully) to fall asleep. It drudges up past experiences, which are usually painful, and constantly niggles at conflicting thoughts. Getting control over your thoughts is how you start to steer them towards goal-oriented thinking, find happiness, and experience inner peace.

Killingsworth (2013) had some interesting findings in his study. "Happiness is indeed highly sensitive to the contents of our moment-to-moment experience," which means what we do now influences our happiness. It would seem that the old maxim of carpe diem is not long forgotten or irrelevant. We should, however, do more than just seize the day—we should seize the moment.

Mindfulness vs. Meditation

You might be forgiven for believing the two are the same, and certainly, they may have similar objectives. However, there are slight differences between mindfulness and meditation.

Mindfulness is when you gently force your mind to look at each moment (Wagner, 2019). You are observing it in an almost detached way as you seek to make peace with what is happening around you. While you are paying more attention, you remove the moment's ability to upset or excite you. Instead, you practice a belief that this moment is precious, but it is already gone, and the next moment is already here. This reduces the hold of negative emotions while balancing positive moments to produce inner calm.

The characteristics of mindfulness, according to Wagner (2019), include:

- Being here, right now
- Letting go of the past
- No longer fantasizing about the future
- Avoiding all forms of judgment
- Gaining control over emotions
- Bonding with yourself

Meditation describes a series of activities aimed at creating mindfulness. While the oldest is rooted in deep inward focusing as is practiced by many religions and philosophical schools such as Vipassana meditation or Buddhism, something as simple as awareness stimulation by gazing at a blade of grass can create mindfulness. Therefore, meditation rather describes various techniques used to achieve mindfulness.

In essence, both meditation and mindfulness are about using your body or your senses to free your mind of daily worry, unhelpful mind-wandering, or negative thought patterns. However, while you can be mindful in a moment, you might not have to be in a meditative state to achieve that inner awareness.

This moment by moment awareness is especially vital in a busy world and a busy life. If you had hours a day to sit and meditate, you would definitely not be a victim to stress or feelings of unhappiness in your life. But what do you do when you don't have that time to sit and chant "Om Shanti" for hours? You meditate just for a couple of minutes a day and do it regularly. Or you choose mindfulness techniques you can do in each moment, quickly reaching that inner focus that allows you to live within the moment without emotion, judgment, or reaction.

Mindfulness techniques are essential steps you take to refocus or retrain your brain to behave differently than you have been doing so far. The more you do it, the more you rewire the neural pathways in your mind, like smokers who need to learn to do something new with their hands when they can no longer hold a cigarette.

Here are some quick ways to retrain your brain to focus inward and not react outwards:

- **Breathe**

You've been doing this for your whole life. Yet, when you are all grown up and stressed out, you forget to do it! To get your mind to focus on you and not what is going on around you, simply breathe. Take a breath in, think, and mentally say, "Inhale." Hold the breath until your body naturally wants to exhale. Now breathe out, thinking and mentally saying, "Exhale." Repeat this until you feel the rhythm of the inhale, hold, and exhale.

Still not convinced. I wasn't either when I started my happiness journey, so I turned to science, and the results are clear: Breathing eases stress, reduces tension, and produces a state of calm focus (Seppälä et al., 2020).

- **Increased Breathing Awareness**

Now that you are breathing again, you can begin to expand your concentration further into your breathing itself. Feel the breath flow deeper into your trachea, down into your lungs, filling bronchial tissue, expanding to push your lungs against your ribcage, pushing your diaphragm further down, and letting your stomach rise outwards. Follow each breath in, then follow each breath out. When you are breathing like this, your focus deepens, and you will not be distracted by what is irrelevant. The dog barking at the neighbor will no longer annoy you, and you will no longer be obsessing about whether your friend really likes you as your whole focus will be on your breathing. Oddly, when you return to regular breathing, you will find yourself filled with peace and calm. You can expect clarity of thought, and you will be able to act instead of reacting.

- **Mindfulness Ritual**

I personally prefer this ritual (Oppland, 2020) to achieve mindfulness in a flash. And, the more you practice it, the better you will get at reaching that inner calm more quickly. This ritual has become instinctual in me now, and when I feel myself becoming stressed or realize my mind is drifting away into the fog of living, I almost subconsciously begin these steps:

1. Sit comfortably and close your eyes, shutting out the outside world for a moment.
2. Think of something pleasant like that stream you went fishing with your dad at as a kid or the smell of freshly baked bread when you were helping your granny.
3. Next, think of a person or favorite pet. Feel the love you have for this living being to fill you as you inhale deeply.
4. Let your mind fill with memories of an event or occasion where you were being thanked. Remember how valued and validated you felt then.
5. Now, let the present seep into your consciousness. Notice how what you had thought was dreadful and simply beyond your abilities to deal with suddenly seems almost insignificant. You are sustained by the positive

energy you created, by the focus you directed inward.

This ritual allows me to use gratitude and the power of good thoughts and memories to counter any negative moments as I engage in them mindfully. I maintain the ability to act in all situations as I trust I have the wisdom (and knowledge gained from all these scientific studies I have shared in this book) to deal with each moment as it arises. Mindfulness and rituals like the above one help to reduce a bad day into moments. We can all deal with a moment, and then the next, and the next.

How Mindfulness Reduces Pain and Negativity

Mindfulness is about you taking control of your brain and making it react in a positive or peaceful way. You do this by taking control of your emotion centers with the activities described above. At first, I also thought that breathing in will do nothing to stop me from being stressed out. Surprisingly, these techniques do help, and they do have the power to reduce pain and negativity. Science backs this as was proved by the 2019 study into whether mindful acceptance can down-regulate pain and negative emotions (Kober et al., 2019).

In the above study, participants who had no previous experience with mindfulness or mindfulness techniques were exposed to images or stimuli that evoked strongly negative emotion or inflicted thoughts of pain. While the participants who didn't practice mindfulness techniques had shown the expected responses to these stimuli—negative emotions, rising blood pressure, increased amygdala responses, and hypertension—those who were told to use mindfulness techniques reacted differently. The group using mindfulness techniques showed a decrease in amygdala responses, indicating a drop in emotional reactivity and decreased blood pressure, and they reported neutral thoughts.

Therefore, mindfulness can reduce pain, negative thoughts, and stress. We can conclude that mindfulness can help us manage moments of our day that would otherwise stop or lower our life satisfaction. In a nutshell, mindfulness can help us be happy. But why does it do this? It changes our brain chemistry.

How Meditation Changes the Brain

While mindfulness is focused on a specific moment, meditation is a much longer, more regulated practice in which the meditator moves through the meditation process to achieve a deeper and more intense state of mindfulness. This distinction is made as meditation and a meditative frame of mind have both been tested in relation to the brain.

In the study by Hölzel at al. (2011), findings reported a notable increase in the gray matter of the brain in the areas of the "posterior cingulate cortex, the temporoparietal junction, and the cerebellum," while other areas are also noted as being affected based on MRI scans. Notably, the hippocampus and the insula are also affected by mindfulness and meditation practices. These two centers are associated with learning, memory, emotional control, and awareness.

The findings of these studies reported by Hölzel et al. (2011) are significant as they indicated that mindfulness and meditation greatly influence how we are able to think, process memories, and control our emotions. Since these changes can be seen in the increase in size of different parts of the brain, this provides concrete proof that you can rewire your brain (hence the increase in size) to think in mindful and more meditative or restful terms about each moment.

Hanson (2011) reports that those who meditate tend to have thicker and better developed areas around the insula. This area, specifically, is involved in "interoception" or the ability to tune into the state of your body. Hence, it is physical and emotional (and mental) awareness.

Hölzel et al. (2011) further indicate that those who regularly practice mindfulness or meditation are also noted to have increased neural plasticity and mental adaptability. As a result, these people recover from stress or trauma much quicker.

Conversely, stress (which is associated with high levels of cortisol, a.k.a the stress hormone) has been proven to yield smaller brains and reduced brain functioning (Echouffo-Tcheugui et al., 2018). Therefore, mindfulness and meditation are effective in reducing stress and boosting brain functioning. I indeed found great benefit in this realization in my life. As soon as I started being more mindful and using the loving-kindness meditation, I felt a vast improvement in my life satisfaction and happiness.

Mindfulness and meditation also improve your health and ability to age well. With meditation, you can slow the rate at which brain cells age and die. While the brain produces thousands of brain cells, especially in the hippocampus, in the process of neurogenesis, it naturally decreases in size due to aging. Hence, any intervention that improves the brain's structural density, through neurogenesis and neuroplasticity, is beneficial in slowing aging (Hanson, 2011). When you meditate, you are using your brain in ways that everyday thinking doesn't achieve. This allows for your brain to stay mentally fit through development and growth.

The Loving-Kindness Meditation

The loving-kindness meditation is "an ultimate form of generous and selfless love towards ourselves and others" (Chowdhury, 2020). Since this meditation centers on loving expression, it is highly effective at improving social integration and encouraging self-acceptance (Hutcherson et al., 2008). By using repetitive loving and positive phrases to heighten awareness and presence, you can improve your mental state, balance your emotions, and improve your physiological health. Emma Seppälä (n.d.) postulates that there are two kinds of loving-kindness meditations: that of receiving and that of giving. Both are necessary to add up to a balanced life and greater life satisfaction or happiness.

A basic loving-kindness meditation may look like this one by Seppälä (n.d.):

- *Become grounded.*

  Sit comfortably, letting your breathing become centered, inhaling powerfully, yet exhaling passively.

- *Receiving loving kindness.*

  With your eyes closed, think about someone who you know loves you very much. This could be a parent, your child, your friends, even yourself. This person could be living or deceased, and you could even choose a favorite pet as an example of a living being who loves you if you don't have anyone else you believe loves you.

  Feel this person or animal standing next to you as you focus inward. Sense their love and best wishes for you coming off them in waves, radiating out to wash over you in a tide of goodwill. You bask in their love and care.

Next, you can add more people or past loved ones to join this person until you are surrounded by all the people who love and care for you. Feel yourself floating in their love. It's quite natural to let a warm smile fill your face at this point. Your body will feel light, and you will feel supported and cared for.

- *Giving or sending loving-kindness.*

In meditation and mindfulness, you are not simply looking inward out of some selfish need. Instead, you are taking care of yourself so that you can take care of the world around you. Having received such blessings and positive energy from the receiving kindness section of the meditation, you can now share that feeling outward. It is best to see this as an endless flow, not like a cup that empties, and then you are left with nothing.

In your mind, picture the person, animal, or even a group of people you want to send your loving kindness to. If you wish, you can even share with those who are no longer living.

Repeat the following sentence several times, thinking it with passion and power:

> *"May you live with ease, may you be happy, may you be free from pain"* (Seppälä, n.d.).
>
> Next, you can change the meditation to contemplate the following thoughts silently and powerfully:
>
> *"Just as I wish to, may you be safe, may you be healthy, may you live with ease and happiness"* (Seppälä, n.d.).
>
> You can change these phrases, making sure they still wish the person or creature safety, comfort, happiness, health, and joy.

Repeating these phrases and visualizing the person healing or being blessed with happiness is a powerful mental exercise. It has been proven scientifically to improve your brain through increased neural plasticity, increased gray matter, and stimulation of emotional happiness. Studies found that the loving-kindness meditation "produced increases over time in daily experiences of positive emotions, which, in turn, produced increases in a wide range of personal resources (e.g., increased mindfulness, purpose in life, social support, decreased illness symptoms)" (Fredrickson, 2008).

Mindfulness and meditation create a mindful presence, and they ground you in the moment. The next step on the road to happiness is to savor each moment, regardless of whether it is positive or negative.

Learning to Savor (and Cope)

Most of us have heard the expression we should savor the moment. While we take this to mean we should value good things when they happen, the reality is that we should savor all moments, whether they are positive or negative. Even a painful moment or experience can offer value when we allow ourselves to fully experience it. If we shut these out, we lose out on learning and growing opportunities in life. By shutting out a negative experience, we also reduce our ability to cope with these.

Life is filled with both positive and negative moments. Savoring good ones now helps to carry us when we are faced with bad ones later. The energy we build from savoring experiences help us cope when we need to. By savoring experiences, we are "regulating the emotional impact of positive events by one's cognitive or behavioral responses," which increases happiness (Jose et al., 2012). The skill of savoring, since it helps us learn to control and know our own emotional and behavioral responses, allows us to better cope when an experience is not pleasant.

I found this concept to be incredibly valuable on my happiness road. Where I had previously tried to avoid and ignore unpleasant experiences or moments (like someone cutting me off in traffic), I now know how to respond peacefully. Instead of getting angry at the guy who almost caused a fender-bender, I simply savor the moment, seeing (without emotion) his car veer in front of mine. With the same calm, which I might enjoy when I'm cruising on the highway with the windows open and the wind in my hair, I am able to apply the brakes and avoid hitting the "offending" car. I don't have to get angry or curse or swerve crazily. Instead, I act in the same calm manner that I do, whether I am enjoying an empty road or navigating rush hour traffic. I savor each moment and act appropriately and without emotional over-involvement.

Savoring a moment (whether good or bad) is also how we obtain happiness. Jose et al. (2012) found that "savoring is an important mechanism through which people derive happiness from positive events." During good events or moments, we are content and at peace. With unpleasant moments, we are soothed by being able to cope effectively, and it is this ability to cope that we savor. Again, this has brought me inner peace and a measure of happiness in my own life.

Taking in (and holding on to) the good, even in a bad situation, is what builds up our brains, improves our abilities, and stimulates our perception of happiness (Hanson, 2011). My golden rule is: If I can feel it, I can cope with it—meaning that I savor all experiences as I know that I am then able to cope with negative ones while enjoying positive ones even more.

A sad reality is that most of us only want the positive experiences, but while we try to avoid negative experiences, they dominate our lives and thinking (Stanley, 2019). When we learn to savor the moment, we increase our enjoyment, experience, and happiness.

The Disruptions of Hedonic Adaptations

While we are meant to savor each moment and be fully present in these as they pass, we are sometimes forced to interrupt our experiences due to disruptions. When a disruption happens, it is without our choice, but sometimes, we choose to interrupt a moment. This could be like taking a break in the middle of an enjoyable movie, or asking the dentist to stop drilling in the middle of a root canal.

Interrupting an experience—pleasant or unpleasant—will intensify it when it continues. Restarting drilling into a tooth after a pause may only intensify the pain, for instance.

The point of all this? When we are experiencing a pleasant experience, we need to be aware that hedonistic adaptation means our enjoyment will plateau. While eating a slice of cake is nice, eating the whole cake in one sitting would be nauseating. However, if you eat a slice of cake today, then take a break and have another slice tomorrow, your enjoyment would be renewed.

"Studies confirm the hypothesis that consumers choose breaks in negative experiences and avoid breaks in positive experiences, despite the finding that these breaks worsen negative experiences and improve positive experiences," according to Nelson and Meyvis (n.d.).

It seems that we chase after thrills, instead of practicing self-control. We should push to finish unpleasant events in one go while choosing to interrupt pleasant experiences to heighten the enjoyment of it. By using intentional interruptions, we can improve our enjoyment and contentment during certain events as we prevent the hedonist plateau from being reached.

Life Appreciation and the Slowdown

"Enjoy it while you can because one day it will be gone." You may have heard something similar to this as a child while growing up. This concept certainly applies to the things that we enjoy but that can end: ice cream melts, parties end, and friends move away.

As an adult, we also have to deal with things running out. Our lives may feel like they are being shaped by shortages: paychecks that don't last, people who die, and marriages that end. And this brings us to another popular saying: "Stop and smell the roses."

We need to slow down if we want to know happiness. While we are living in a world that rushes from point A to B, we are missing out on a great deal that has the power to change our lives for the better. This happens because we are simply in such a rush that we don't slow down to really pay attention.

Once we accept that experiences end, we are more likely to focus and enjoy them, whether that experience is your life, going on holiday, or meeting a friend. Kurtz (2008) in her study found support "for the counterintuitive hypothesis that thinking about an experience's ending can enhance one's present enjoyment of it." Since we know that the experience is ending, it changes our behavior, and we experience greater well-being. This knowledge that the experience is limited motivates us to make the most of it, and as a result, we enjoy it all the more.

If we knew with real certainty that something would end, like if you knew the day of your death, would you enjoy life more? Most things we can repeat, but the things that actually matter, we can't. We can't live again, nor can we meet a best friend for the first time again. Knowing that those things only happen once, or that they have a limited time, has the power to enrich our enjoyment and appreciation.

Accepting death, for instance, has the power of enriching your life. Studies among terminally ill patients revealed a surprisingly high happiness quotient present despite the knowledge that these participants had of their own death (Griffin, 2017). This does not mean we need to rush out and contract a terminal illness to be happy. Instead, we need to become mentally aware that everything is limited. Nothing lasts forever. The terminally ill have a unique perspective on the finite nature of life. While their time on earth may be running out, they often choose to slow down and focus inward, realizing what holds value and what is trivial. There is great contentment to be found in this approach.

Paying attention makes you aware of what your power to influence things really is. Where you may simply have had life happen to you, it is in your power to affect life and to influence what happens to you. You certainly control how you respond to the business of living. Every breath you take is a choice. Deciding to get up in the morning is a choice, and being happy or unhappy are also choices.

Slowing down, seeing your choices, and realizing your power to take action instead of following reactions can be liberating. Thinking about something ending can enhance your experience of it, whether that thing is life, your relationships, or even your job.

An interesting exercise in mindfulness and existentialism that has recently gained traction among self-help and business schools is to write your own obituary. While this may seem morbid and would seem to have no place in a book about happiness, this technique is powerful at making you realize what will bring you contentment.

Studies support that the obituary writing technique is a way to slow down, really understand yourself, and map out what your happiness journey may look like. "The experience of completing one's own obituary begins with emotional discomfort followed by a transformative shift in the direction of a greater sense of acceptance, appreciation, and awe toward the possibilities of living the life one envisions" (Bland, 2020).

This transformative shift is what the slowdown and inward focus or introspection are all about. Once you realize that things end, you begin to feel a growing forward momentum or a desire to achieve what you envision. This is a powerful force to create happiness with. Remember: happiness doesn't just happen; it is created—by YOU!

The obituary writing exercise works like this:

- *Your name*

Start by writing your name. Visualize what it will look like when it's engraved on your tombstone one day. Use this as a way to let yourself dive into the experience of loss.

- *Your legacy*

Write in a few sentences what you've done to make your world a better place. Be specific, and really look at your life.

- *How you will be remembered*

Create a list of all the things you will most be remembered for. These things could be big things, and they could also be little things that you are proud of. Also include the people who will remember you for these things.

- *Who?*

Write a couple of sentences in which you explain who you really were. Dive in and find every aspect of who you are, what makes you who you are, and how did you become who you are?

- *Yes and no*

In life, you may know exactly what you want, but the answer to questions usually becomes a "Yes." This happens because we are conditioned to please others. However, you need to defend what you want, and it can become harder to stand firm and say "No." What do you want to say "No" to? List some things you have been doing that you actually wanted to say "No" to.

This may include going out with questionable friends, letting people use you, or engaging in activities you find boring simply because it makes other people happy.

This activity will help you slow down and focus inward. Participants in studies where this activity was done reported an increased awareness of the beauty of life, and they also recorded an improvement in their overall happiness. Once you know, I mean really know, that things end, the fear of this end fades, and you can learn to flow with life.

The Science of Flow Theory

This theory has nothing to do with "going with the flow" where you just throw in the proverbial towel and have a "so what" attitude. This flow is when you are so entirely focused and involved in something that the world fades. Scientists call it "flow" since it is intense and incredibly satisfying, and it produces a heightened enjoyment that is unrivaled. Like a river that flows endlessly, when you are experiencing a state of flow, time seems to loop or stop, and you simply live in that moment (Miller, 2020).

When we are in a state of flow, we are so involved (actively creating) with what we are doing that we are unaware of time, and the world passes by unnoticed, but we experience more meaning. Both positive or negative behavior can create the flow condition. It is about the intensity with which we are engaged in the activity we have chosen.

“When a person can organize his or her consciousness so as to experience flow as often as possible, the quality of life starts to improve” (Csikszentmihalyi, 1990). We can then invest our focus in mental processes that add value to our lives instead of sifting through random thoughts that detract from the experience and destroy happiness. Flow brings mindfulness, and mindfulness brings flow—the two are linked. With flow, “thoughts, intentions, feelings and the senses are focused on the same goal” (Csikszentmihalyi, 1990). When you are in a state of flow or mindfulness, you notice all details, and you are able to focus on your goals, measure your progress, plan contingencies, and push yourself for even bigger goals.

Indeed, studies among college students found that those who were successful in engaging in an activity with sufficient flow experienced the most positive affect (or became positive minded). Regularly achieving flow (especially when you have specific goals) is then a great way to improve your life with positive thinking. This allows you to cultivate a positive attitude (Rogatko, 2009). The results of a state of flow include inner motivation, focus and improved moods, and ultimately, you achieve better performance (Kasa and Hassan, 2013).

Gaining flow is about focus or our ability to pay attention—it encompasses all that I have discussed with you in this chapter. We need to stop mind-wandering. Only when we use mindfulness and meditation to deepen our inward thought, strengthen our awareness, and sharpen our focus, can we begin to cultivate powerful attention abilities. Savoring each moment, we can start to step off the freight train that most of us are stuck on in our lives, and we can take control of our lives by being present. We need to slow down. Apply the brakes and start paying attention to each moment of our lives because tomorrow it might be gone. When we can successfully do this, we will be able to create happiness and embrace the flow.

These levels of introspection and attention span require a certain degree of self-honesty. When we can admit to ourselves who we are, what matters to us, and focus fully on each moment of our lives, we can begin to discover contentment.

Hello, I'm Present, or Am I?

Grab your journal for this. You are about to discover whether you are mindful, attentive, and present in each moment of your life. Again, there is no wrong or right for any of these. Simply work through each activity, then write in your journal about the experience. Self-reflection is a means to insight and awareness, and these can help you create happiness.

- **The Raisin**

Find a raisin. Just an ordinary raisin. Sit quietly, holding the raisin in the palm of your hand. Let your eyes take in the shape, patterns, texture, coloring, and lines of the raisin. Imagine the raisin being etched on the backs of your eyelids.

Next, touch the raisin, feeling the squishy nature of the little fruit. It may be only a shriveled-up grape, but this raisin is fascinating! Feel it, letting the smooth, sticky texture of the raisin awaken your fingertips.

Now, smell the raisin. Allow the summery sweetness of the raisin to fill your nostrils, setting your mouth watering as you begin to imagine what that raisin may taste like. When you really know what this humble raisin looks like, you can take the final step and allow the raisin to sink into your tongue, filling your mouth with flavor.

In your journal, write about each of these senses. Record how you felt, smelled, and touched the raisin.

When you have written about the raisin, you can use the same investigation method that you used on it to explore another object, person, or experience. Use this method to focus inward on your perceptions and awareness of each moment.

- **Snapshot**

In this technique, imagine that you are walking around with a camera, taking snapshots of everything around you. However, do not use a real camera. Instead, purposefully choose a random image from your surroundings and focus on that image as if it is a picture. This allows you to "freeze" a moment to be evaluated and experienced in more depth.

Begin small. Choose something in your home to look at like it is captured in a photo. Let the image, colors, lines, shapes, interactions, and whatever else is involved in your selected "picture" imprint into your mind. Take as long as you want to look at this moment you have "frozen."

Now, write about what you see, what you feel, and what you experience. Try to capture as much detail as you can in your journal. Describe the feeling of inner peace that fills you as you reach a state of flow, where the outside world fades away, and all that exists is your "picture."

My favorite moment like this was watching a loved one who was busy enjoying the opening of a present. I could have watched them rip off the brightly colored gift wrapping paper for all eternity. There were such beauty, peace, and perfect tranquility in that moment. All that existed was the pure joy on the gift receiver's face. On that particular day, I achieved flow. Even thinking back to that moment still brings me contentment and peace.

- **Step by Step**

This is a powerful and highly beneficial exercise to do. Choose a time of day when the area around your neighborhood is quieter. Take a walk. On this occasion, don't disappear into your Spotify account or hide behind sunglasses. Instead, look at the world around you. Move in and through that world one step at a time.

With each step, choose one thing to focus on for five seconds. Even counting from one to five can help you focus on the selected thing. Lose yourself in the details. Then, step forward into the next moment, choosing something else to focus on.

When you have concluded your walk, spend a few minutes writing about the experience. Reflect on the feelings you experienced, how you saw the time, and any other thoughts related to the experience you may have.

When you start experiencing mindfulness, you may be a little self-conscious. It is probably a whole lot different from what you have been doing until now. Allowing yourself to experience things with mindful awareness requires honesty. Trusting yourself to be real and authentic with each moment in your life is a huge responsibility. Still, on this journey you will discover the liberation of self and real happiness creation.

Chapter 8

Be Honest and Content

Happiness is when what you think, what you say, and what you do are in harmony.

~ Mahatma Gandhi

"Honey, does my butt look big in this?" The words that any partner dreads, which (out of necessity) forces him to think up an appropriate white lie to try and convince his dearest that their plus-size butt really does look okay in two-sizes-too-small jeans.

While the above scenario has been the butt of many jokes, it is a reality most of us can relate to. Something happens and, if we spoke the truth, it would hurt someone we love. To protect their feelings, we lie. There are many reasons why we lie. To get out of trouble, we lie. To avoid embarrassment, we lie. To make things easier, we lie. The reasons for lying are numerous, but mostly, our lies can be grouped as either being a white lie or a black lie.

White lies are told to protect someone, and black lies are told to hurt someone or protect ourselves. The results are not always the same. White lies can actually make us feel a small sense of happiness when we realize our white lie has made someone else feel good, as in a prosocial (or white) lie (Zanette et al., 2016). Prosocial lies can increase bonds when the truth comes out as the person being lied to may appreciate that the liar was trying to protect them. However, antisocial or black lies (lies meant to hurt someone or serve our self-interests) were shown in the Zanette et al. study to be marked with signs of contempt, and ultimately, these lies destroy social bonds when the truth comes out.

Lying or being dishonest in life can become a habit if we are not aware of it. Studies (Garrett et al., 2016) found that lying for personal gain has the effect of decreasing the activity of the amygdala in the brain. This is the area associated with moral coding and judgment. Participants in the study were rewarded for telling lies that cost someone else something. With time, their lies became larger and more frequent to obtain the personal reward of money. Therefore, antisocial (or personal gain) lies can begin to take a strain on your brain, and they can become a habit. The lure of money (or reward) distracts us from living here and now and being accountable for our actions right now.

Science indicates that lying can be bad for your health too (Ten Brinke et al., 2015), but more on the health implications of lying a bit later. When we lie to hurt someone or promote our own needs, we are negatively affecting our happiness (and theirs). You may feel "good" when you achieve the aim of your lie, but ultimately, the cost of maintaining that lie will cancel out any gain. When you have to keep lying straight in your head, you can't live in the moment, and you will not be able to live peacefully or contentedly. Happiness will be the cost of your lies.

The Truth Shall Set You Free

It is a reality that lying, even making up white lies, is draining. You have to constantly focus on remembering who you told what, and it requires a sustained (and draining) effort to maintain the falsehood. Whatever your reason for keeping up the lies—out of a fear of being caught out or to keep from hurting someone else—lying is a wasted effort, and it will hurt the person being lied to.

But why do we lie when it requires that much effort and can be so damaging to ourselves and to those we lie to? Studies (Choshen-Hillel et al., 2020) have found that we also lie to appear honest when the truth seems to overly favor us. This may seem like a conundrum, but essentially, we lie when we believe people won't believe us. If we fear people will think of us as dishonest when the truth may seem overinflated, we may underplay the truth or lie. For instance, when you have met someone famous, you may lie about it to prevent people from thinking you are bragging.

Some of the other reasons for lying that affect our ultimate happiness include (Ekman, 2020):

- **To avoid punishment**

  We easily see this with children who will lie about who broke a window to avoid getting punished for the misdeed. However, it is also evident in adults. In a marriage or relationship, one partner may lie to the other about infidelity to avoid "punishment."

- **To get a reward you don't qualify for**

  As adults, we are sometimes tempted by a reward we don't deserve. We might lie about our skills or interests to get into a job or club we don't qualify for.

- **To be liked and admired**

  To get the attention of others, we may also be tempted to lie. We could pretend to be someone we're not to gain friendship and companionship. This is perhaps the most draining and potentially most damaging kind of lying.

  Other reasons why people lie include protecting someone else from punishment, protecting yourself from suffering physical harm, avoiding embarrassment, keeping your privacy, and getting information and power out of someone else.

Lying is draining. There is always a good chance that the truth will come out. This necessitates that we need to maintain a front of lies to keep the truth hidden. You need to constantly recall what you said to whom, and you need to always control your reactions, facial expressions, and actions to maintain the false facade you have constructed. In the end, at some point, there will be spillage hinting at those you are lying to, that you are dishonest. When the truth does come out, the damage will be irreparable. In short, nobody likes to be lied to. Once trust has been broken, the chances of repairing it are slim.

Ironically, people still believe that antisocial lying can be for their partner's good. Those engaging in infidelity may try to assure themselves that they lie to protect their partner. They believe that their partner can't handle the truth. As a result, the lies in the relationship escalate. What does this look like in reality? Partners "reassuring" each other that they are happy within the relationship and that all their needs are being met. However, since their needs are not met, they may begin to look outside the relationship for satisfaction. Still, they keep lying to each other because they believe their partners can't handle the truth. Research has refuted that people can't handle the truth (Levine & Cohen, 2018).

Levine and Cohen found that people mispredict the consequences of honesty. People believe that it is better to lie, but telling the truth would have yielded a better end result. Within relationships, telling your partner lies because you believe they can't deal with honesty will lead to severe mistrust. However, admitting to your partner that you are unhappy and there are things in the relationship you don't like and want to change, can build trust and improve the relationship bond. Ultimately, studies found that "communication and moral values shape well-being" (Levine & Cohen, 2018).

Essentially, telling the truth can build relationships, add to your happiness, and it is far less work! Lying is a dangerous game of deception, and it is a lot of work. The payoff of lying is far less than you might think; instead, the cost of dishonesty could be more than you can bear.

Honesty Improves Health

In a study conducted by Kelly and Wang (2012), participants were divided into two groups. One group was instructed to consciously stop all lying, while the second group received no instructions. Both groups were monitored with health checks and polygraph tests on a weekly basis as well as regularly completing relationship assessments. The results found that those who stopped lying showed a significant drop in blood pressure, better heart health, and they reported less health-related concerns as well as a general improvement in life satisfaction or happiness. Their relationships also did much better than the neutral or control group.

The cost of lying is not only directed at the person being lied to. It also affects the liar significantly.

Leanne ten Brinke et al. (2015) found that maintaining a lie has severe costs to your physical health.

- **Dishonesty takes up mental functioning**

To lie to someone means you need to remember something that isn't real. This influences not only your memory centers but also your executive centers, as you have to consciously keep that knowledge at the front of your mind.

Not sure how this works or why it would be tiring? Spending today only answering to the name SARAH and pretending that you like cats can give you a taste of this fatigue. When people talk to you, introduce yourself every time by this name. Only react when they call you by this name. Research information about cats, tell people about a fictional cat named Bobby. Oh, and if your lie is discovered by someone who doesn't know you, there is a $500 fine that you must pay to a charity, which the person you lied to can choose.

While it might be interesting at the beginning, by the time you reach lunch, you will begin to feel the strain. While you are focused on being SARAH, you are unable to relax or live in the moment. You are constantly thinking of how to convince people you are really SARAH. Taking your blood pressure may present a picture of you being highly stressed. You fear being found out, and you think of ways to convince people all the time. This means you have to remember everything you said to everyone, or the game is up, and you'll be out of $500! Your stress levels will skyrocket.

- **Dishonesty leads to greater cortisol productivity and stress reactivity**

Since lying is stressful, your cortisol production will increase. In turn, this will elevate your stress levels and paranoia even more. You will fear that those who know the real you will let something slip, and as a result, you may begin to avoid the people who really know you. Isolation will lead to feelings of unhappiness and fear.

- **Dishonesty increases physiological effects and arousal levels**

Stress (from lying) is associated with an elevated heartbeat, higher blood pressure, and increased body temperature, and you could risk having a stroke, aneurysms, and other stress-related conditions. At the very least, you may suffer headaches, indigestion, and a lack of appetite. This is not a picture of a happy person.

- **The same may happen to the one being lied to**

When you take the time to notice the person you are lying to, you will begin to see a mirroring of your symptoms in them. The person who doesn't know you are not SARAH will also suffer physiological reactions as they begin to doubt the veracity of your act.

- **Dishonesty leads to negative health conditions**

Your health, and the health of the person who you are lying to, will rapidly decline. While you may experience this to a lesser extent with the act being only a day in length and not involving any damaging intentions, you can imagine what the effect of lying will be over a longer period and for more nefarious reasons. Imagine lying about something for a year or more to someone. If you felt stressed and panicked in just a day, how will you feel after a year?

Ultimately, lying isn't worth it. Even white lies can cost you dearly. Telling someone you like their hairstyle, for instance, can have lasting repercussions when they discover that you were lying.

Better then to avoid saying anything when you can't tell the truth. But how do you go about telling the truth when you don't want to hurt someone? How do you make truth part of your happiness journey?

Being Honest, Being Happy

It is so easy to lie, especially when you have done so repeatedly. Maintaining lies takes more effort, as I pointed out in the above discussion. Practicing honesty can be an act of persona liberation. Freedom from lying can help boost your happiness. Getting there when you start on the path of truthfulness and happiness can take some deep questioning. These questions can help you decide whether you should be honest, keep quiet, or use a prosocial lie:

1. If I say this, will I be hurting anyone? Should I rather withhold the truth to spare someone's feelings?
2. Would my truth help or hurt this person? Could they grow from hearing the truth, or would it serve no purpose?
3. If I was in the same situation, would I want the truth or a white lie?
4. Keeping the truth to myself, would that be an act of compassion, or do I choose the easy way

out by saying nothing because it may be awkward?

By considering these questions before you speak, you can begin to make decisions about what you say, your truthfulness, and the impact of your words on others and yourself. Lying for the sake of lying or personal gain will not lead to happiness.

Are You Honest?

Using your journal, you can reflect on your words and deeds. This is where you face yourself, decide if you were truthful or deceptive. If you have been lying habitually and want to change this to improve your well-being and happiness, then you will find benefit from these activities:

- **THINK**

This is a life-skill exercise that has found its way into most classrooms. Using the acronym THINK, you pause for a few seconds before speaking or acting to think.

Is it TRUE?

Is it HELPFUL?

Is it IMPORTANT?

Is it NECESSARY?

Is it KIND?

This way of thinking before you speak (or lie) will help you decide whether you should speak or remain silent. It enables you to determine whether the truth would be helpful or hurtful in the scenario you are facing. Prosocial or white lies can be exhausting, and you shouldn't underestimate people's capacity to process truth (even when that truth might not be what they want to hear). Telling your friend her choice in today's outfit isn't ideal may help her improve her dress code, or it could hurt her. You will have to find a way to be honest, without being brutal.

- **Pins and Needles**

Lying to others can make you feel like you are sitting on pins and needles. It is draining and physically harmful. It can cost you friends, and it can devastate people's ability to trust again. A life of lies is not a happy one.

Using a page in your book, write the name of the person you are worried about lying to. Each night, think back over the day, and for *every* lie (or maintenance of a lie) that you spoke, take a pin and stick it into the page. Remove the pin, noticing the hole that remains in the page. That hole will always be there. Record the "injury" by writing the date next to the hole.

This is a record of lies, and it is up to you to rectify it. Keep a separate page for each month per person. Notice whether the holes become fewer as you page per month. When you can apologize for a lie, you can fill up the hole with some correction fluid.

At the bottom of each page, write a little pledge about not telling lies, and if you are unable to apologize to the persons you lied to, you can use your journal to speak out about your lies and why you lied.

The aim of this activity is not to beat yourself up. Instead, you can use it proactively by mentally seeing the page's image with needle holes to help remind you to stay on track and replace lies with happiness.

- **No More Lies**

While you can control yourself, you can't control others. Avoiding people who you suspect of being liars can help you keep some peace in your life, as interacting with them always comes with a measure of suspicion. But what do you do when you know yourself to be a habitual liar? Take the liar test. When you go for a polygraph, you are not only measured by the machine that reads your physiological signals. The interviewer also monitors you for other signs of deceit. You can use this to keep yourself in check.

- Do you look the person in the eyes you are about to speak to?
- Are you struggling to speak or stuttering?
- Did your tone of voice change?
- Do you apologize or make profuse excuses?
- What is your body posture?
- Do you feel uncomfortable?

These reflective questions will help you track yourself for deception. If you notice any of these signs, STOP. Hold yourself accountable for what you are doing or about to do. Write about these questions in your journal. Why do you feel compelled to do something that falls into the lying category? Now that you know lying has no payoff except putting your health, relationships, and happiness under strain, is there any reason to do it?

With the truth now firmly in mind, it is time to look at your life and how you are going to steer it back towards happiness. To do so, you will need some goals.

Chapter 9

Goals and Why You Need to *ACT* on Them

When obstacles arise, you change your direction to reach your goal; you do not change your decision to get there.

~ Zig Ziglar

While most of us know what a goal is in layman's terms, I want to be really specific here. A goal is something in the future that has meaning to you, which you want to achieve. But a goal is also a plan or a series of steps on how to reach a desired outcome. Therefore, it is a direction to take, being both—a starting point and a destination.

Goals can help us feel good. They can help us get the positive energy to move forward in life. Goals bring us a purpose, and they make us strive for accomplishment, which gives us happiness. Even just striving towards a goal can already bring a sense of happiness to us.

We learn about life from the goals we choose to pursue. While we may run into obstacles while we try to reach our goals, we learn to change direction, and we learn perseverance. By wisely choosing goals that are within reach, but encourage us to grow, we set ourselves up for happiness.

What Do Goals Do?

All of us have a goal in mind. Often, this may be a massive monster of a goal, like becoming the next president of the United States, but goals don't have to be big to matter. Even the smallest step can create a ripple that changes your life. If you are someone who has been bedbound with depression, then setting it as your goal to get up in the morning may be a big enough goal to change your life.

Goals give direction. They help us know where we are going, and since we can tick them off our daily, weekly, monthly, or even annual to-do list, we are enriched with a feeling of accomplishment. We need goals to help us realize we are making progress in life, instead of simply spinning wheels on the spot.

When we are engaged in the pursuit of goals, we are acting in the best interest of our well-being. Results from the Macleod et al. (2008) study provided support for the view that "goal setting and planning skills have a causal link to subjective well-being." The good news is that these well-being enhancing skills can be learned. So, working on our planning and goal setting skills can offer a vast potential to develop our lives and well-being.

Setting Positive Goals

Procrastination is one of the reasons why people accomplish nothing. Instead of launching their forward movement, people doubt, and they are reluctant or demotivated to start with their pursuit of happiness. Setting positive and achievable goals will inspire and motivate you to have a purpose. With this approach, your goals will become specific, and you will have the strength to follow through.

Having a personality and life approach that are positive, we enjoy our lives more. With a "dispositional optimism" (Wrosch & Scheier, 2003), we are able to adapt to changing circumstances without letting go of our original goal. When you have a dispositional optimism, you generally expect that good things will result from something, or you anticipate a favorable outcome. You tend to favor an optimistic life view and not a negative one. Your ability to cope in a changing world is largely part of your skills and disposition, and these, in turn, affect your ability to remain happy despite when goals seem unachievable.

"Implementation intentions are interpreted to be powerful self-regulatory tools for overcoming the typical obstacles associated with the initiation of goal-directed actions" (Gollwitzer & Brandstätter, 1997). The reason you are engaging or pursuing a goal is what drives you. Don't lose sight of that. It will help you overcome obstacles that may crop up, and it is what fueled your need to satisfy this goal. It is your meaning; don't lose it.

Positive goals may help you stay true to your course and achieve success in life and in happiness. The trick is to choose goals that are within reach but novel and exciting enough to inspire dedicated commitment. Your life satisfaction is based on achieving goals, not failing at them. Hence, setting positive goals will lead to happiness as you are using these goals to set you up for success.

When setting your goals, consider the following:

- *Are your goals taking you towards something positive you want to attain?*

Avoid goals that are directed at avoidance. Studying hard to avoid your father giving you a hiding is a negative goal; however, studying hard since you want to become a doctor and help people is a positive goal.

- *When your goal goes off track, do you run and hide, give up, or proactively step up?*

Life rarely goes exactly as planned, and when you go off the rails or your goals become endangered, it is up to you to find ways to solve the problems and overcome the obstacles. Shutting your eyes and hoping for the best is a negative response where you give up your power to act. Always keep the ball in your court and act.

- *Are you making peace with the goal gremlins?*

If you stare at the negative in life, you will be stuck in place. There will be challenges along the way. Instead of avoiding them or dreading them, embrace them, change your course to accommodate them, and keep heading in the general direction of your goal. Re-adjust and step up; don't retreat and step back.

Powerful Habits

Can habits help you become happy? Since habits are just actions that repeat themselves, they can be used to help you make progress on your happiness journey as they get you going. Progress can only happen when you take action, and conversely, when you take action, you make progress. This cycle of acting to achieve progress and progress leading to action is what we experience when we set goals, reach them, set new goals, and so on (Pychyl, 2008). Goal achieving through action can become a habit.

So, how do you use habits to help you achieve your goals? Since powerful habits could include having the mental discipline to act (as opposed to a negative habit to procrastinate or lounge around doing nothing all day), they are the opposite of the goal-minded paradigm. We need to decide to act and make this decision a habit. When it becomes our habit, we will start doing it without needing to first find the motivation.

Let's face it—sometimes we are low on motivation. However, when we are already in the habit of acting, we do so with minimal motivational requirements. It becomes less about whether we find something interesting (novel) and more about whether it is necessary and important. Habits are also not something you have to actively think about. When you are walking to work, which is a habit, you don't have to think about where you are going—your subconscious mind already knows. This frees up your mind to focus on other more meaningful pursuits such as goal setting and future planning.

Some successful habits I have cultivated that helped me on my happiness journey include:

- **Focus on the NOW**

While you may think mindfulness and presence aren't habits, they can become a habitual behavior. I make it my habit to focus on what I am busy with right now. Though I may have many goals to achieve, I pick one and focus on that exclusively in the time I have available. This brings me to my next habit ...

- **Use TIME wisely**

If you want to be effective at reaching your goals, then you need to be proactive about time management. Happiness will not magically appear just because you wish to have it. You will need to MAKE time to achieve your goals. I am conscious of every minute of the day, and my habit is to use that time wisely and to be productive. Even if I only have five minutes available, I use it wisely. You can get a lot more done in five minutes than in five hours if you are wise and focused.

- **Keep TRACK**

I monitor my progress in my goals. It is a habit that is not directed at really seeing what I achieved, but it is rather about understanding what I have done, where I will go next, and how I will get there. Keeping track of things is not about measuring; it is about reflecting, learning, and being mindful (Clear, n.d.). It is less about saying something is done and more about seeing how I got there. This creates satisfaction. Remember, happiness isn't a destination–it's a journey, and you can find it in every step of the way.

The Dangers of Comparisons

Don't try to keep up with the Joneses. Trying to satisfy outside expectancies or keep up with other goal setters instead of focusing on your own progress can become a major obstacle. It is YOUR goal, not THEIRS. "The more we internalize and identify with a goal by understanding the value behind it or even simply the importance of the task, the more likely we are to act autonomously" (Pychyl, 2008). Identify with your goal, compete with yourself. The world can take care of itself. You only need to take care of your goals, your motivations, and your actions.

"Everyone is on their own path, and we all do what's right for ourselves, in our own time" (Fabian, n.d.). You have your path, and looking over at what your neighbor is doing the whole time will just cause you to miss seeing an obstacle in your way, and as a result, you will trip yourself up. When you are competing with someone else, you will constantly be aware of what you lack instead of what you have. This brings on a case of "what you lack, you attack." There is no need to waste energy on confrontation. Instead, focus on your path, your goals, and your success.

If you allow someone else to set your goals, you will not identify with your goals, and in the end, you will not be able to internalize those goals nor strive to achieve them. Before you decide on a goal, make sure it's your goal and not something dictated by your friends, colleagues, family, or environment. These questions (Camarote, 2016) can help:

1. Do YOU want this?
2. Does this goal fit in with everything else you have wanted in your life?
3. Do you have the resources to pursue this goal?
4. Do I need to trade off or simplify another goal to reach this one?

5. If it's not my idea, what does the suggesting person get out of it?
6. Why do the people around me think it's a good idea, and do I think it's a good idea?
7. When this goal is done, what is next? Do I want what comes next?

Always check that the face in the goal mirror is your own and not that of other people. It is your life, and it is your goal. Trying to run the race in someone else's shoes will only give you blisters, so focus on what you need, desire, want, and believe in.

What Goals to Pursue

You are never too old to set another goal, or to dream a new dream.

~ C. S. Lewis

Deciding on what pursuit is worthy of being YOUR goal is something you shouldn't rush into. Committing to a goal will require your time, resources, and energy, so make sure it's the right goal for you. Having a sounding board is a useful way to get an outside and unbiased opinion. This is probably one of the main reasons why people have a need to open up and share their thoughts and experiences. We may sound like we are asking for advice, but really, we just need to vocalize our own take on things.

Like C. S. Lewis said, you aren't too old to dream a new dream. If you want to take up triathlon training since you've always wanted to, you can do so even in your later years of life. There are no limits to what you can achieve. But when you start out, having realistic goals can help you make better progress. This doesn't mean letting go of your goal; instead, it means breaking big goals into smaller ones. After all, the ultimate goal is the happiness you gain from the pursuit of your goals.

To start off, you can begin to vocalize your goal. It is part of the planning process. If you have a trusted friend or family member, they can be your sounding board, or if you like, you can consult a mentor for advice and feedback. If none of those are available, you can use your journal to sound out your goal, question your motives, plan your steps, and reason your decision out.

Using questions will help ground you in the decision-making process of goal setting. If you have no idea of how to set a goal or what you should consider as an avenue of goal pursuit to look into, then you might consider the different areas of your life (Mind Tools, n.d.). Evaluate your happiness in each, deciding whether you need to focus or set a goal for happiness in any of them. Once you set your goals, you'll start noticing opportunities for their achievement—you can only find something when you know what you are searching for. Consider:

- **Your Career**

Have you found your passion in your career? Did you reach the level of proficiency you are happy with? If you are falling short of the mark or seeing your job as just a job, then you may want to consider taking on extra responsibilities or studying further, or even a career change to help motivate you and bring happiness to your life. Remember that your job takes up around 35% of your total waking hours (Thompson, 2016). Choosing to be unhappy for roughly 35% of your time is unwise, so finding or building (with goals) a career that brings you contentment (and not just financial rewards) is important for your life satisfaction. If you recall Chapter 2, money can only bring you happiness up to a certain threshold; after that, it has minimal benefit to your overall life satisfaction and happiness. Perhaps you should take classes, register for an online course to build your job skills, or even consider moving to a different company. Change is often a goal in itself.

- **Finances**

Most of us wish we had more money, or we wish we had more time for the same amount of money. Your goal could be to learn about time management, find better investment goals, or increase your earnings with side hustles. Be sure your financial goals are realistic and in line with the other aspects of your life. Money doesn't solve all problems, but it can surely create them. Your money goals shouldn't cost you happiness. Use your money goals to create happy moments and experiences.

Suppose you want money so you can afford to take your family on holiday. In that case, your goal might be to save enough, to take on a second job long enough to save the money you need, or work with your financial planner to calculate whether you can afford to take a loan from a bank for the holiday. Be specific about what you need from your finances and set appropriate goals. Winning the lottery isn't a goal.

- **Level of Education**

Many people wish they had achieved more in terms of their education. Perhaps the opportunities weren't there in your earlier life. If this is an area where you feel frustrated, then you could consider what you would like to learn and plan how you will achieve these goals. Be sure that "fame" isn't your goal. Education is about learning, not about writing a few letters before or after your name. Find out what will benefit you in terms of education. Do you need a bachelor's or master's degree to earn more at work, or can a series of short courses and more experience achieve the same goal?

- **Family**

Are you lonely? Perhaps you've been so career driven that you've never had the time to start your own family? Maybe you are married and are unable to have children? Whatever your family situation, if you are not fully satisfied, it is up to you to decide how and what to make into a goal. Perhaps you should make it your goal to meet people and join a club or go on dates more often? If you are married, maybe you should talk to your partner about adoption if you are unable to conceive? Decide which changes in your family life will make you happy and turn those into goals.

- **Artistic Side**

As human beings, we all need to create something. Creation is more than just painting or drawing. It is about putting yourself into something and feeling a sense of achievement when we have made that thing. Your artistic side could find satisfaction in a range of creative things, from baking cakes to cooking, to rebuilding old cars and landscaping. If your life is feeling dull, you may need to find an artistic avenue to express yourself in. Make it your goal to learn about new and exciting things to create. Watch some YouTube videos, take a few classes, or join a few clubs. As a bonus, these goals will also bring you greater social contact and connection.

- **Personal Attitude**

Do you sometimes have quiet moments when you think, "Damn, I'm a really grumpy person?" Chances are that your attitude needs some revision. Becoming bitter or feeling dejected happens without us even noticing it, but luckily, you can set it as your goal to work on a better attitude. You could start by applying the practices from this book. Or you could also go to therapy, learn about personality and commitment theories, or you could attend classes in mindfulness and self-awareness.

- **Physical Conditioning**

Many of us look in the mirror and cringe. We become flabby and crabby, especially with aging. While this is bad for our health, we also feel down-trodden when we let our bodies decay. Joining a gym or making it your goal to go walking every day are healthy goals to set.

These goals should be about what you want, what will bring you health, and what will make you happy. They should also be reasonable if they are to succeed. Should you decide to make extreme cage fighting your first goal (because you saw it on TV), but you hardly ever leave your couch, then you might be setting yourself up for failure. Instead, you might decide you want to make basic fitness your first goal, then follow this by taking up boxing, followed by a few local competitions, and ultimately, you might become an extreme fighter.

- **Entertainment**

Humans have the need to have fun and be entertained. Our entertainment might include socializing and relaxation activities. If your life is feeling boring, then you might consider finding a hobby a goal. Or you could also regularly check out what your local theaters and cinemas have to offer.

- **Public or Social Service**

When we take care of others, we take care of ourselves too. Many people find great enjoyment and happiness from serving others, engaging in charity work, or reaching out through community work. Doing social service or caring for a goal can bring great joy and purpose into your life.

If you have read about these parts of your life and still feel stuck, don't despair. Many of us are often stuck, knowing something is missing but not knowing what. Your journal activities for this chapter will help you get unstuck.

My Goals, My Happiness

Pull your journal closer, and let's get started.

1. Visual Inspiration

Sometimes we don't know what we want or what will make us happy. Asking others isn't the way to go. Using your journal, some magazines, and loads of glue—collect some images, words, and anything else that pops out at you to create some visual logs or visual collages to inspire you.

Don't overthink this, and don't try to make meaning out of it immediately. Simply collect things that you notice, and then leave the pages for a few days. Then, armed with a favorite cup of tea and some magic markers, begin to circle things in your pages that appeal to you. Write them down on the next page. It might include things like skydiving, swimming along the Great Barrier Reef, and doing a few African safaris. These could be grouped together as "adventure."

Does your life need more adventure? Now ask yourself how you can make adventure your goal. It can be in the form of a holiday, but it can also be to take up a sport or hobby that brings you adventure.

Once you know what will thrill you, plan it, break it into actionable steps, and DO IT!

2. Plan YOUR Goals

Once you have a couple of goals written down, you may want to carefully consider them. Use your journal to record your thoughts as you work through these five questions:

- **Do your goals have a structure to them?**

  Decide on how your goals can be broken into smaller sections that are easily manageable and will boost your sense of accomplishment, creating inner courage in you.

- **How will you measure your progress?**

  Setting a goal is essential, but it also includes how you will track your progress. Do you have levels of achievement, or could you have a specific end result that will confirm the goal has been reached?

- **Can you take action to reach your goal?**

Sometimes, we bite off more than we can chew. If your goal is too big, you will struggle to reach any real sense of accomplishment. You will be setting yourself up for failure. Make sure your goals are within reach of your resources, time, energy, knowledge, and motivation.

- **Did you decide on a reward?**

Any goal is a bit like a race. You reach the finish line, and you want a reward. Whether it's a medal, a certificate, a lovely meal out with friends, or even a pat on the back—you need a reward. The best rewards are the ones that come from us. You should allow yourself to enjoy your own approval and not seek that of others.

- **Did you plan for the right time?**

Sometimes our goals are just scheduled at the wrong time in our lives. This can be tricky because you don't want to set them aside and eventually discard them entirely. When you realize that right now is not maybe the best time for a goal, then you should have the endurance and commitment to revisit that goal in a short while, determining whether it is now the right time for the goal. Don't give up just because now isn't right.

With this inquisitive line of thinking, you can decide how to plan for your goal. If you can't track your progress, then there will be a lack of motivation. Make yourself accountable for the action steps you plan. Don't say, "I'll do this." Say, "I'll do this by ___."

Most people struggle with achieving their goals as they want some miracle or magic mood to guide them. They want to have a boss who tells them to do this or that and tell them once they have reached the goal. We really can't be blamed; after all, we mostly live and work in a hive culture that suits most traditional employment forms well. But goals are about YOU. They are about achieving YOUR goals, and you can't wait for instructions or moods. YOU have to set the goal, draw up the action items, plan the schedule. YOU have to decide when your goal is reached.

Chapter 10

Don't Wait for Mood—Do It *NOW!*

Comfort zones are where dreams go to die.

~ Regina King

We are creatures of habit, and we like to live in easy ways. Anything that is hard work, we seem automatically preprogrammed to avoid. Or do we really seek to avoid work? While you may have sunk low into your comfort zone, this is where dreams die. If you have a dream or a goal you want to reach, then you need to step outside of your comfort zone, learn, grow, and achieve.

How often have we heard someone say, "I'll do it later. I'm not in the mood now." This is the excuse of the weak and uninspired. Yes, you may think that's harsh, but it is a reality. You can make excuses, or you can get busy pursuing your goals. The *choice* is

YOURS. If you are going to hide behind mood, then you will likely have expectations of failure. Yip, you will probably not even try.

No, I am not painting a picture of failure for you. Instead, I want you to forget about your mood, forget about excuses or reasons why you can't do something. You can! You really can. All it takes is courage and the willingness to take risks. No, don't quit your job. You don't have to take drastic action like that, although you may later decide that it is time to make a career change. The goal here isn't to throw in the towel. It's to step up, to get into the spotlight of your ambitions, and shine.

Finding Courage

Not all of us are naturally born with bucket loads of courage. Indeed, most of us are quite timid by nature. While your upbringing may have added to your ability to step up and show courage, especially when you believe you are standing for something morally upright, being brave isn't the norm.

Oh, sure, you get those kids in the neighborhood who can never seem to go fast enough, jump high enough, or risk their lives enough. You know, the kids that the angels work overtime on. And research has tried to explain this in terms of them being a "Type T" personality. People with this genetic predisposition seem to actively seek thrills and danger. Such individuals possess "fewer dopamine receptors in their brains" (Kets de Vries, 2020), which means they need more stimulation or thrills to get the emotional payoff from being active and taking risks. While the rest of us are happy to watch extreme sports, they have to be out there *doing* it.

To pursue and achieve your goals, you will need courage, but not that type of courage. So, relax and put down the phone. There's no need to arrange for more life insurance.

Instead of seeking insurance, you need assurance. Self-assurance. Albert Bandura, a famous psychologist, believed that we could achieve anything we set our minds to as long as we had self-assurance or belief in our abilities. He called this *self-efficacy* (Kets de Vries, 2020). With a healthy dose of high self-esteem and self-belief, you can accomplish anything you set your mind to. All that is needed is to get out of your comfort zone and work at your goal, even if doing so is scary.

But what do you do when you have low self-esteem? How can you be brave when you are almost hanging on by your fingernails from fearing your boss? What chance do you have of actually pursuing the goal of changing careers?

It's simple; you have to find courage. It isn't some mythical gift that the gods forgot to bless you with—it's a skill, and you can grow yours. When you know what is important enough to use your courage on, you can learn in small steps to be courageous.

You should focus on developing courage when it comes to speaking up to assert your boundaries, and you should have courage when you need to decline something you know isn't right for you. It takes courage when you have to admit you failed at something. Working at your goals takes courage.

To develop better courage, you need to know what you stand for, what you believe in, and what you seek. In small steps, you can build up and reinforce your self-esteem, and you can learn to trust your own abilities. Nobody wakes up one morning with enough confidence to conquer the world. You work at it. With every challenge, you are testing yourself, seeing how much further you can push today.

Courage is within your reach when you allow yourself to grow braver. You manifest courage in your life in small steps, achieving the courage to tackle the bigger goals. Having courage doesn't mean you are without fear, and while you may think brave people are fearless, they only face their fears from one moment to the next.

Being mindful and present in each moment will also help keep your mind on track and stop mind-wandering that could dredge up thoughts of failure. If you doubt that you have the courage to step up and work at your goals, then simply tell yourself the following affirmation:

I only need to have enough courage for this moment. I will take care of the next moment once I am there.

This affirmation, when spoken, comforts you that you needn't worry about the whole picture. You only need to be strong and courageous right now.

Taking Risks

We live in a world that oftentimes appears to be scary, and for the most part, we try not to take risks. If we did, we wouldn't have health insurance, life insurance, and death benefits. Those all point to the fact that we want to be in control and be safe—and there's nothing wrong with that.

However, when we want to change something, we need to let go a little. We need to put in the work and see where we land. This is a risky business. While you can break a goal down into smaller steps to prepare as much as possible and reduce the risk substantially, in the end, you have to take a leap of faith.

That faith is in yourself, in a higher power, in preparations you made to the best of your abilities, and in being right in your goal-setting paradigm. But, let's face it—leaping is scary. That's why people generally tend to scream when they jump off high things.

It is also invigorating, which is also why people jump off high things. While our comfort zone is safe, it is also boring. Taking a calculated (and well-prepared for) risk is exhilarating, and we feel alive. The thrill we feel when we have succeeded in a risky situation is brought on by endorphin activity, but it is also because of the intrinsically motivated success we enjoy. We have succeeded! Victory! There is no better feeling, whether that feeling comes from running the Boston Marathon, swimming with sharks, or getting a bank loan for the small start-up that you have set as your goal. Success tastes sweet.

The Reality of Risks

I hate the saying, "expect the best, plan for the worst." It makes me feel like people are always anticipating the worst thing to happen. Oh, sure, there will be failures along the way. If setting goals and reaching your happiness was easy, we would all do it without even batting an eye. But, in reality, risks are usually not as bad as you anticipate.

You may have been conditioned to believe that anything that steps outside of the norm is risky, dangerous, foolish, and will end in disaster. That's why you have probably been spending your life in the relative safety of your comfort zone. Have you been happy there? Did nothing bad ever happen to you while you were hiding from life in your comfort zone?

If you answered YES to the above, you have probably been living on another planet. The reality is that bad things do happen, but guess what? You can adapt to them, and you can cope with them, and if you allow yourself to learn from them, you will be a few steps closer to your happiness.

While you may be planning for the worst, you should also allow yourself that optimistic view that it won't be as bad as you anticipate. We humans tend to always get a little melodramatic about the risks connected to our goals. If you have a goal to achieve a better education, what's the worst that could happen? Perhaps you don't complete your degree studies? Even though that might happen, you would still be a few years of study (and acknowledgment) closer to a degree than you were without that goal.

Nobody ever feels like they want to take a risk. It's something that scares us. Yet, when you are reaching for the stars to achieve your happiness, you have to learn to fly, and that includes the possibility of falling. Being prepared, breaking your goals into smaller steps, and carefully considering how to make this goal as safe as possible before you leap, will minimize risk and maximize the chance of success. You wouldn't just leap. You would take some flying lessons, plan for the best day to do this, invest in a parachute, and only then would you jump. All of those steps require action. TAKE it NOW!

A Happier You

Reaching for your goals, achieving them, and enjoying contentment will produce a YOU who is so much *more*. The pursuit of happiness will make you more content, more optimistic, more caring, more capable, more committed, more devoted, more present, and more everything!

You will change for the better.

Change, in any form, is scary. Embrace the new you. Don't be afraid to keep pushing ahead, to keep making decisions that are in your best interest, and to create your own happiness.

While you stand here on the cusp of adventure, of goals, of your happiness, you may have a few doubts still circling your mind, telling you to stop being silly, to give up, to be realistic, and to let go of this foolishness. Take a moment to listen to that voice, that inner doubt, that old version of you. Hear it growing fainter, fading away as you listen. You have already changed. The knowledge of this book has changed you. All that is needed now is action.

When I wrote about life appreciation earlier, I mentioned that when you know something ends, you appreciate it more. If you still have any doubts that are holding you from taking action, I wanted to remind you that life ends. Those who really realize this, such as the terminally ill, have left us a legacy of insight with their "regrets of the dying," as recorded by palliative carer Bronnie Ware (n.d.):

"I wish I'd had the courage to live a life true to myself, not the life others expected of me."

"I wish I hadn't worked so hard."

"I wish I'd had the courage to express my feelings."

"I wish I had stayed in touch with my friends."

"I wish that I had let myself be happier."

Don't let regret be your future. Your happiness is within reach—you create it. Your life, your body, your mind, your heart, and your courage are enough to undertake any pursuit and any goal that will bring you within the realm of your happiness. You have a happy mind, a happy life.

New Beginnings

To live is the rarest thing in the world. Most people exist, that is all.

~ Oscar Wilde

When I set out to find my happiness, I had no idea where I would end up. I had created a goal for myself: to scientifically understand happiness, learn how to create it, and discover a way to share it with others. My journey towards happiness started outward, reading scientific studies ad nauseam and finding all the pieces of the puzzle that was my life, but then I began to move inward. I learned to take charge, to reach into my own abilities, and to create my own life and happiness.

I have shared my journey from start to finish, except there is no finish, no row of magical lights that flash when I reach point X. The finish is what inspires the journey. I realized I would die. Scary as it was, I embraced and accepted death, and I realized my ability to set goals and achieve them would one day cease.

While you have a life now, while you have a body, a mind, and the possibilities to decide on goals, you can take action. You can create your happiness, and now you have all the tools and knowledge on how to do it. All you have to do is start actively creating yours.

In closing, I would like to leave you with a brief recap on happiness, but unlike other books that usually restate what you have learned, I would like to gift you with a few affirmative statements to remind you of the knowledge you have been enriched with:

- I am not born with happiness that I have lost; I create my own happiness as I live my life.
- Money won't make me happy, but experiences I can buy with it can bring me happiness.
- My body, when healthy, helps my mind make happiness my reality.
- In building relationships with others, I can share my happiness and reciprocate connection.
- My kindness has the power to change my life, enrich my goals, and bring happiness into every moment.
- Gratitude brings me perspective and harmony within my actions.

- I appreciate every moment while being present and mindful.
- Honestly, with pure intent, I set my goals and strive for positive action.
- My goals and habits place me in control of my happiness.
- The time is now. The action is mine.

You have the power to create your happiness today. There is no reason to wait, no challenge too big to overcome, and no goal that you can't reach when it comes to your happiness creation. When your life becomes rich with positive emotions, good relationships, and a sense of purpose, you become ready to accomplish all the goals of your heart.

◆◆◆

If the information presented in this book can help you even in the slightest way possible, then I'm more than excited. In the case you enjoyed *Happy Mind, Happy Life* and found it helpful, **please consider leaving a review**.

Even if your review is just a sentence or two—it makes all the difference and is greatly appreciated. That helps the book find its way to those who might need to read it. Thank you!

Please choose one depending on the country you are based in:

- Scan Here to Leave a Review on Amazon.com

- Scan Here to Leave a Review on Amazon.ca

- Scan Here to Leave a Review on Amazon.co.uk

About the Author

Barbora Centik is an author, entrepreneur, and a mental health advocate with a passion for helping others learn how to live happier, more fulfilling lives. She honestly doesn't know where she lives—she loves to travel and says that her "home is where the heart and suitcase are."

After repeatedly suffering from stress and anxiety—and discovering that her degree and shiny career don't actually lead to fulfillment—Barbora became determined to uncover the real truth behind happiness. Now, she's fascinated with the science behind well-being, and she's determined to bring practical, science-backed strategies to the world. She hopes to touch the lives of her readers, arming them with the tools they need to transform their mindsets and build happier, more fulfilling lives.

Publisher's Note

If you want to be the first to hear about our new releases, from this and other authors, giveaways, and limited offers (free e-books and audiobooks), follow us on Facebook or Instagram @8BCpublishing. Feedback for the author or publisher is welcome at hello@8bcpublishing.com.

References

Ackerman, C. E. (2020). *What is happiness and why is it important?* Positive Psychology. https://positivepsychology.com/what-is-happiness

Aesop. (n.d.). *Aesop quotes*. Brainy Quotes. https://www.brainyquote.com/quotes/aesop_109734

Aknin, L. B., Dunn, E. W., Helliwell, J.F., Biswas-Diener, R., Nyende, P., Barrington-Leigh, C. P., Burns, J., Kmeza, I., Ashton-James, C. E., and Norton, M. I. (2013). Prosocial spending and well-being: cross-cultural evidence for a psychological universal. *Journal of Personality and Social Psychology*, 104(4), 635-652. https://doi.org/10/1037/a0031578

Allen, S. (2018). *The science of gratitude*. Greater Good Science Center. https://ggsc.berkeley.edu/images/uploads/GGSC-JTF_White_Paper-Gratitude-FINAL.pdf

Bland, A. M. (2020). The existential obituary writing technique for emerging adults:

thematic and content analyses. *The Humanistic Psychologist.* Advance Online Publication. https://doi.org/10.1037/hum0000176

Boothby, E., Clark, M. S., and Bargh, J. A. (2014). Shared experiences are amplified. *Psychological Science,* 25(12). https://doi.org/10.1177/0956797614551162

Brown, J., and Wong, J. (2017). *How gratitude changes you and your brain.* Greater Good Magazine. https://greatergood.berkeley.edu/article/item/how_gratitude_changes_you_and_your_brain

Buddha. (n.d.). *Buddha quotes.* Brainy Quotes. https://www.brainyquote.com/quotes/buddha_101052

Camarote, R. (2016). *How to make sure your goals are yours and not someone else's.* Inc. https://www.inc.com/robin-camarote/how-to-make-sure-your-goals-are-yours-and-not-someone-elses.html

Carlessi, A. S., Borba, L. A., Zugno, A. I., Quevedo, J., and Réus, G. Z. (2019). Gut microbiota-brain axis in depression: the role of neuroinflammation. *European Journal of Neuroscience.* https://doi.org/10.1111/ejn.14631

Carpenter, D. (2020). *The science behind gratitude (and how it can change your life).* Happify Daily. https://www.happify.com/hd/the-science-behind-gratitude/

Choshen-Hillel, S., Shaw, A., and Caruso, E. M. (2020). Lying to appear honest. *Journal of Experimental Psychology: General,* 149(9), 1719-1735. https://doi.org/10.1037/xge0000737

Chowdhury, M. R. (2020). *What is loving-kindness meditation? (Incl. 4 Scripts).* Positive Psychology. https://positivepsychology.com/loving-kindness-meditation

Clear, J. (n.d.). *Goal Setting: A scientific guide to setting and achieving goals.* James Clear. https://jamesclear.com/goal-setting

Corcoran, K. (2015). *Rewiring the brain for happiness: the neuroscience of happiness,* Part 2. The Table. https://cct.biola.edu/rewire-your-brain-neuroscience-happiness-part-2

Csikszentmihalyi, M. (1990). Flow: The Psychology of optimal experience. *Research Gate*. https://www.researchgate.net/publication/224927532_Flow_The_Psychology_of_Optimal_Experience

Curry, O. S., Rowland, L. A., Van Lisa, C. J., Zlotowitz, S., McAlaney, J., and Whitehouse, H. (2018). Happy to help? A systematic review and meta-analysis of the effects of performing acts of kindness on the well-being of the actor. *Journal of Experimental Social Psychology*, 76, 320-329. https://doi.org/10.1016/j.jesp.2018.02.014

Dickens, C. (n.d). *Charles Dickens quotes*. Good Reads. https://www.goodreads.com/quotes/21915-reflect-upon-your-present-blessings----of-which-every-man

Echouffo-Tcheugui, J. B., Conner, S. C., Himali, J. J., Maillard, P., DeCarli, C. S., Beiser, A. S., Vasan, R. S., and Seshadri, S. (2018). Circulating cortisol and cognitive and structural brain measures: the Framingham heart study. *Neurology*, 91(21). https://doi.org/10.1212/WNL.0000000000006549

Ekman, P. (2020). *Why do people lie? 9 motives for telling lies.* Paul Ekman Group. https://www.paulekman.com/blog/why-do-people-lie-motives

Epley, N., and Shroeder, A. (2014). Mistakenly seeking solitude. *Journal of Experimental Psychology: General,* 143(5), 1980-1999. https://doi.org/10.1037/a0037323

Fabian, S. (n.d.). *When I stopped competing, I set myself free.* Tiny Buddha. https://tinybuddha.com/blog/stopped-competing-set-myself-free

Fowler, J. H., and Christakis, N. (2008). Dynamic spread of happiness in a large social network: longitudinal analysis over 20 years in the framingham heart study. *BMJ.* https://doi.org/10.1136/bmj.a2338

Fredrickson, B. L., Cohn, M. A., Coffey, K. A., Pek, J., and Finkel, S. M. (2008). Open hearts build lives: Positive emotions, induced through loving-kindness meditation, build consequential personal resources. *Journal of Personality and Social Psychology*, 95(5), 1045-1062. https://doi.org/10.1037/a0013262

Gandhi, M. (n.d.-a). *Mahatma Gandhi quotes.* Brainy Quotes. https://www.brainyquote.com/quotes/mahatma_gandhi_150726

Gandhi, M. (n.d.-b). *Mahatma Gandhi quotes.* Brainy Quotes. https://www.brainyquote.com/quotes/mahatma_gandhi_105593

Garrett, N., Lazzaro, S. C., Ariely, D., and Sharot, T. (2016). The brain adapts to dishonesty. *Nature Neuroscience,* 19, 1727-1732. https://doi.org/10.1038/nn.4426

Gollwitzer, P. M., and Brandstätter, V. (1997). Implementation Intentions and Effective Goal Pursuit. *Journal of Personality and Social Psychology,* 73(1). htpps://doi.org/10.1037/0022-3514.73.1.186

Good Therapy. (n.d.). *Guilt.* https://www.goodtherapy.org/learn-about-therapy/issues/guilt

Gordts, E. (2014). *Professor Richard J. Davidson: 'Happiness is a skill that can be learned.'* Huffpost. https://www.huffpost.com/entry/richard-j-davidson-davos_n_4636683?guccounter=2

Grant, A. M., and Gino, F. (2010). A little thanks goes a long way: explaining why gratitude expressions motivate prosocial behavior. *Journal of Personality and Social Psychology*, 98(6), 946-55. https://doi.org10.1037/a0017935

Griffin, A. (2017). *Dying people are surprisingly happy about it, study finds*. Independent. https://www.independent.co.uk/news/science/dying-people-happy-terminal-illness-study-cancer-als-death-north-carolina-a7768636.html

Hanson, R. (2011). *How to trick your brain for happiness*. Greater Good Magazine. https://greatergood.berkeley.edu/article/item/how_to_trick_your_brain_for_happiness

Hatfield E, Cacioppo JT, Rapson RL. (1993). Emotional Contagion. *Current Directions in Psychological Science*. Cambridge University Press. 2 (3). 96-100. https://journals.sagepub.com/doi/abs/10.1111/1467-8721.ep10770953?journalCode=cdpa

Hershfield, H. E., Mogilner, C., and Barnea, U. (2016). People who choose time over money are happier. *Social Psychological and*

Personality Science, 1-10. https://doi.org/10.1177/1948550616649239

Hersh, E. (2018). *The best 11 apps to track your happiness in 2019.* Positive Routines. https://positiveroutines.com/track-your-happiness-apps

Hillman, C., Erickson, K. I., and Kramer, A. F. (2008). Be smart, exercise your heart: exercise effects on brain and cognition. *Nature Reviews Neuroscience,* 9(1), 58-65. https://doi.org/10.1038/nrn2298

Hölzel, B. K., Carmody, J., Vangel, M., Congleton, C., Yerramsetti, S. M., Gard, T., and Lazar, S. W. (2011). Mindfulness practice leads to increases in regional brain gray matter density. *Psychiatry Research,* 191(1), 36-43. https://doi.org/10.1016/j.pscychresns.2010.08.006

Howes, M. J., Hokanson, J. E., and Lowenstein, D. A. (1985). Induction of depressive affect after prolonged exposure to a mildly depressed individual. *Journal of Personal Social Psychology,* 49(4), 1110-3. https://dpoi.org/*10.1037/0022-3514.49.4.1110*

Hutcherson, C. A., Seppälä, E. M., and Gross, J. J. (2008). Loving-kindness meditation increases social connectedness. *Emotion, 8*(5), 720-724. https://doi.org/10.1037/a0013237

Jebb, A. T., Tay, L., Diener, E., and Oishi, S. (2018). Happiness, income satiation and turning points around the world. *Nature Human Behaviour,* 2, *33-38.* https://doi.org/10.1038/s41562-017-0277-0

Jose, P., Lim, B. T., and Bryant, F. B. (2012). Does savoring increase happiness? A daily diary study. *The Journal of Positive Psychology,* 7(3), 176-187. https://doi.org/10.1080/17439760.2012.671345

Kahneman, D., and Deaton, A. (2010). High income improves evaluation of life but not emotional well-being. *Psychology and Cognitive Sciences,* 107 (38), 16489-16493. https://www.pnas.org/content/pnas/107/38/16489.full.pdf

Kasa, M., and Hassan, Z. (2013). Antecedent and consequences of flow: lessons for developing human resources. *Procedia - Social and*

Behavioral Sciences, 97, 209-213. https://doi.org/10.1016/j.sbspro.2013.10.224

Kelly, A. E., and Wang, L. (2012). *Lying less linked to better health, new research finds.* American Psychological Association. https://www.apa.org/news/press/releases/2012/08/lying-less

Kets de Vries, M. F. R. (2020). *How to find and practice courage.* Harvard Business Review. https://hbr.org/2020/05/how-to-find-and-practice-courage

Khazaee-Pool, M. (2015). *Effects of physical exercise programme on happiness among older people.* Research Gate. https://doi.org/0.13140/RG.2.1.3124.0160

Killingsworth, M. (2013). *Does mind-wandering make you unhappy?* Greater Good Magazine. https://greatergood.berkeley.edu/article/item/does_mind_wandering_make_you_unhappy

King, R. (n.d.). *Regina King has the best advice for when you're feeling stuck.* E!. https://www.eonline.com/news/1081586/regina-king-has-the-best-advice-for-when-you-re-feeling-stuck

Kober, H., Buhle, J., Weber, J., Ochsner, K. N., and Wager, T. D. (2019). Let it be: mindful acceptance down-regulates pain and negative emotion. *Social Cognitive and Affective Neuroscience,* 14(11), 1147–1158. https://doi.org/10.1093/scan/nsz104

Kogan, N. (2020). *The magic of a good night's sleep*. Happier. https://www.happier.com/blog/the-magic-of-sleep

Koo, M., Algoe, S. B., Wilson, T. D., and Gilbert, D. T. (2008). It's a wonderful life: mentally subtracting positive events improves people's affective states, contrary to their affective forecasts. *Journal of Personality and Social Psychology*, 95(5), 1217-1224. https://doi.org/10.1037/a0013316

Kumar, A., Killingsworth, M. A., and Gilovich, T. (2020). Spending on doing promotes more moment-to-moment happiness than spending on having. *Journal of Experimental Social Psychology*, 88(103971). https://doi.org/10.1016/j.jesp.2020.103971

Kurtz, J. L. (2008). Research report: looking to the future to appreciate the present. the benefits of perceived temporal scarcity. *Pomona College: Psychological Science*, 9(12), https://doi.org/https://doi.org/10.1111/j.1467-9280.2008.02231.x

Le Roy, B. (2016). *Is kindness contagious?* World Tribune. https://www.worldtribune.org/2016/02/is-kindness-contagious

Levine, E. E., and Cohen, T. R. (2018). You can handle the truth: mispredicting the consequences of honest communication. *Journal of Experimental Psychology: General,* 147(9), 1400-1429. https://doi.org/10.1037/xge0000488

Lewis, C. S. (n.d.). *C. S. Lewis quotes*. Good Reads. https://www.goodreads.com/quotes/812245-you-are-never-too-old-to-set-another-goal-or

Lima-Ojeda, J. M., Rupprecht, R. and Baghai, T. C. (2017). "I am I and my bacterial circumstances": linking gut microbiome, neurodevelopment, and depression. *Frontiers of Psychiatry,* 8(153). https://doi.org 10.3389/fpsyt.2017.00153

MacLeod, A. K., Coates, E., and Hetherton, J. (2008). Increasing well-being through teaching goal-setting and planning skills: results of a brief intervention. *Journal of Happiness Studies: An Interdisciplinary Forum on Subjective Well-Being*, 9(2), 185-196. https://doi.org/10.1007/s10902-007-9057-2

MedlinePlus. (2020). *Depression.* https://medlineplus.gov/genetics/condition/depression

Meyer, C. (2018a). *5 Science-backed reasons why being social is good for your health.* Second Wind Movement. http://secondwindmovement.com/social-health-seniors

Meyer, C. (2018b). *Fight loneliness with these 9 simple tactics – part 1.* Second Wind Movement. http://secondwindmovement.com/fight-loneliness

Miller, K. D. (2020). *The psychology and theory behind flow.* Positive Psychology. https://positivepsychology.com/theory-psychology-flow

Mindtools. (n.d.). *Personal goal setting: planning to live your life your way*. Mind tools. https://www.mindtools.com/page6.html

Mogilner, C. (2010). The pursuit of happiness: time, money, and social connection. *Psychological Science,* 21(9), 1348-1354. http://doi.org/10.1177/0956797610380696

Morres, I. D., Hatzigeorgiadis, A., Stathi, A., Comoutos, N., Arpin-Cribbie, C., Krommidas, C., and Theodorakis, Y. (2018). Aerobic exercise for adult patients with major depressive disorder in mental health services: a systematic review and meta-analysis. *Depression and Anxiety,* 36(1), 39-53. https://doi.org/10.1002/da.22842

Nehlig, A. (2013). The neuroprotective effects of cocoa flavanol and its influence on cognitive performance. *British Journal of Pharmacology,* 75(3), 716-727. https://doi.org/10.1111/j.1365-2125.2012.04378.x

Nelson, L. D., and Meyvis, T. (n.d.). *Interrupted consumption: adaptation and the disruption of hedonic experience.* New York University.

http://pages.stern.nyu.edu/~lnelson0/Nelson%20and%20Meyvis.pdf

Newman, J. (2018). *Is social connection the best path to happiness?* Greater Good Magazine. https://greatergood.berkeley.edu/article/item/is_social_connection_the_best_path_to_happiness

Oppenheim, J. (n.d.). *James Oppenheim quotes.* Good Reads. https://www.goodreads.com/quotes/194556-the-foolish-man-seeks-happiness-in-the-distance-the-wise

Oppland, M. (2020). *13 Most popular gratitude exercises & activities.* Positive Psychology. https://positivepsychology.com/gratitude-exercises

Otake, K., Shimai, S., Tanaka-Matsumi, J., Otsui, K., and Fredrickson, B. L. (2006). Happy people become happier through kindness: a counting kindnesses intervention. *Journal of Happiness Studies,* 7(3), 361-375. https://doi.org/10.1007/s10902-005-3650-z

Pennock, S. F. (2020). *The hedonic treadmill – are we forever chasing rainbows?* Positive Psychology.

https://positivepsychology.com/hedonic-treadmill

Pishva, N., Ghalehban, M., Moradi, A., and Hoseini, L. (2011). Personality and happiness. *Procedia - Social and Behavioral Sciences*, 30, 429-432. https://doi.org/10.1016/j.sbspro.2011.10.084

Purse, M. (2020). *Norepinephrine's role in treating mood problems*. Very Well Mind. https://www.verywellmind.com/norepinephrine-380039

Pychyl, T. A. (2008). *Goal progress and happiness: how to decrease procrastination and increase happiness*. Psychology Today. https://www.psychologytoday.com/us/blog/dont-delay/200806/goal-progress-and-happiness

Reynolds, G. (2018). *Even a little exercise might make us happier*. New York Times. https://www.nytimes.com/2018/05/02/well/move/even-a-little-exercise-might-make-us-happier.html#:~:text=Small%20amounts%20of%20exercise%20could,of%20exercise%20may%20be%20helpful

Rogatko, T. P. (2009). The influence of flow on positive affect in college students. *Journal of Happiness Studies,* 10(2), 133–148. https://doi.org/0.1007/s10902-007-9069-y

Rowland, L., and Curry, O. S. (2019). A range of kindness activities boost happiness. *Journal of Social Psychology*, 159(3), 340-343. https://doi.org/10.1080/00224545.2018.1469461

Schocker, L. (2014). *Here's a horrifying picture of what sleep loss will do to you*. Huffpost. https://www.huffpost.com/entry/sleep-deprivation_n_4557142?guccounter=1&guce_referrer=aHR0cHM6Ly93d3cuYnVzaW5lc3NpbnNpZGVyLmNvbS9pbmZvZ3JhcGhpYy1zaG93cy1pbXBhY3Qtb2Ytc2xlZXAtZGVwcml2YXRpb24tMjAxNC0oP3I9REUmSVI9VA&guce_referrer_sig=AQAAAA57m7a6-j0fpUwVypzuD83vP3R072s5leuWX99zTysrZB1m92WJ0GIduidQ3I3Nlic3tyM4Vg_y5TruxWQ0skj_hgolAJ9rXRbMmZaT5e3JdbNQPVqxOIjAkWnPUqJe47FkYd1tza50E-e9ugiuSCffu5QLadgRruFDw6KJ2HT1

Seppälä, E. (n.d.). *Loving-kindness meditation.* Greater Good Magazine.

https://ggia.berkeley.edu/practice/loving_kindness_meditation

Seppälä, E., Bradley, C., and Goldstein, M. R. (2020). *Research: why breathing is so effective at reducing stress*. Harvard Business Review. https://hbr.org/2020/09/research-why-breathing-is-so-effective-at-reducing-stress

Simpson, J., & Weiner, E. (eds.) (1989). Happy. *Oxford English Dictionary*. Oxford: Oxford University Press. http://www.oxforddictionaries.com/definition/english/happy

Slyepchenko, A., Carvalho, A. F., Cha, D. S., Kasper, S., and McIntyre, R. S. (2014). Gut emotions - mechanisms of action of probiotics as novel therapeutic targets for depression and anxiety disorders. *CNS Neurol Disord Drug Targets,* 13(10), 1770-86. https://doi.org/10.2174/18715273136661411300205242

South University. (2018). *Why being social is good for you*. Counseling and Psychology. https://www.southuniversity.edu/news-and-blogs/2018/05/why-being-social-is-good-for-you#:~:text=As%20humans%2C%20social%20interaction%20is,important%20component%20of%20adult%20life

Stanley, J. (2019). *The science of savoring*. Live Happy. https://www.livehappy.com/science/science-savoring

Stoerkel, E. (2020). *Can random acts of kindness increase well-being?* Positive Psychology. https://positivepsychology.com/random-acts-kindness

Sun, J., Harris, K., and Vazire, S. (2019). Is well-being associated with the quantity and quality of social interactions? *Journal of Personality and Social Psychology.* https://doi.org/10.1037/pspp0000272

Taylor, M. (2019). *The negative impact of hitting the snooze button*. Early Bird by Ameris Sleep. https://amerisleep.com/blog/negative-impact-snooze-button/#:~:text=We%27ve%20established%20that%20hitting,for%20some%20major%20health%20problems

Ten Brinke, L., Lee, J. J., and Carney D. R. (2015). The physiology of (dis)honesty: does it impact health? *Current Opinion in Psychology, 6,* 177-182. http://doi.org/10.1016/j.copsyc.2015.08.004

Thompson, K. (2016). *What percentage of your life will you spend at work?* ReviseSociology. https://revisesociology.com/2016/08/16/percentage-life-work

Thoreau, H. D. (n.d.). *Henry David Thoreau quotes.* Brainy Quotes. https://www.brainyquote.com/quotes/henry_david_thoreau_379350

Ullrich, W., Gais, S., Haider, H., Verleger, R., and Born, J. (2004). Sleep inspires insight. *Nature,* 427. https://msu.edu/course/psy/401/Readings/WK9.PresentA.Wagner%20et%20al.%20(2004).pdf

Wagner, P. (2019). *Meditation and mindfulness; methods for lasting peace.* Gaia. https://www.gaia.com/article/meditation-vs-mindfulness-methods-mindsets-for-lasting-peace?gclid=Cj0KCQiAhZT9BRDmARIsAN2

E-J1HsyORLOq8B4QKLM_A_9-sc94s-gq0lcXHr3-DkAEm87jzkWB7rk0aAtBfEALw_wcB

Walker, J., Kumar, A., and Gilovich, T. (2016). Cultivating gratitude and giving through experiential consumption. *Emotion,* 16(8), 1126-1136. http://dx.doi.org/10.1037/emo0000242

Walsh, C. (2008). *Money spent on others can buy happiness*. The Harvard Gazette. https://news.harvard.edu/gazette/story/2008/04/money-spent-on-others-can-buy-happiness

Ware, B. (n. d.). *Regrets of the dying*. BonnieWare.com. https://bronnieware.com/blog/regrets-of-the-dying

Watson, S., and Cherney, K. (2020). *The effects of sleep deprivation on your body*. Healthline. https://www.healthline.com/health/sleep-deprivation/effects-on-body

Williams, P. (2013). *Happy*. Lyrics.com. https://www.lyrics.com/lyric/30024711/Pharrell+Williams/Happy

Wilde, O. (n. d.). *Oscar Wilde Quotes*. Good Reads. https://www.goodreads.com/quotes/2448-to-live-is-the-rarest-thing-in-the-world-most

Wrosch, C., and Scheier, M. F. (2003). Personality and quality of life: the importance of optimism and goal adjustment. *Quality of Life Research, 12,* 59-72 https://doi.org/10.1023/A:1023529606137

Wu, J. (2020). *Which of these four attachment styles is yours?* Scientific American. https://www.scientificamerican.com/article/which-of-these-four-attachment-styles-is-yours

Yong, S. J., Tong, T., Chew, J., and Lim, W. L. (2020). *Antidepressive mechanisms of probiotics and their therapeutic potential.* Frontiers of Neuroscience. https://doi.org/10.3389/fnins.2019.01361

Zanette, S., Gaoa, X., Brunet, M., Stewart Bartlett, M., and Leea, K. (2016). Automated decoding of facial expressions reveals marked differences in children when telling antisocial versus prosocial lies. *Journal of Experimental Child Psychology,* 150, 165-

179.
https://doi.org/10.1016/j.jecp.2016.05.007

Ziglar, Z. (n.d.). *Zig Ziglar quotes*. Good Reads. https://www.goodreads.com/quotes/57566-when-obstacles-arise-you-change-your-direction-to-reach-your

www.ingramcontent.com/pod-product-compliance
Lightning Source LLC
LaVergne TN
LVHW091408190726
843491LV00006B/1330

9783949152047